The Rise of Christianity

Other Books in the Turning Points Series:

Turning Points

IN WORLD HISTORY

The Rise of Christianity

Don Nardo, *Book Editor*

David L. Bender, *Publisher*
Bruno Leone, *Executive Editor*
Bonnie Szumski, *Series Editor*

Greenhaven Press, Inc., San Diego, California

Every effort has been made to trace the owners of copyrighted material. The articles in this volume may have been edited for content, length, and/or reading level. The titles have been changed to enhance the editorial purpose.

No part of this book may be reproduced or used in any form or by any means, electrical, mechanical, or otherwise, including, but not limited to, photocopy, recording, or any information storage and retrieval system, without prior written permission from the publisher.

Library of Congress Cataloging-in-Publication Data

The rise of Christianity / Don Nardo, book editor.
    p.   cm. — (turning points in world history)
  Includes bibliographical references and index.
  ISBN 1-56510-963-5 (lib. : alk. paper). —
ISBN 1-56510-962-7 (pbk. : alk. paper)
  1. Church history—Primitive and early church, ca. 30–600. 2. Church history—Middle Ages, 600–1500. I. Nardo, Don, 1947– . II. Series: Turning points in world history (Greenhaven Press)
BR162.2.R56 1999
270.1—dc21
                                        98-17499
                                          CIP

Cover photo: Victoria & Albert Museum/Art Resource, NY

Printed in the U.S.A.

Contents

Chapter 2: The Growth and Spread of Christianity

Testament. Many candidates were considered and rejected along the way.

Chapter 3: The Problems of Christianity

Chapter 4: The Triumph of Christianity

system and the pagans, their numbers steadily declining, found themselves increasingly on the defensive.

breakaway Protestant groups, remained the predominant faith of Europe and of the lands colonized by European states. The Christians went on to face many challenges, including the rise of rationalism, science, and communism. But they prevailed and are today more numerous than ever. Thus, the legacy of early Christianity was the creation of a faith that managed to survive and grow until it became the most widely practiced religion in world history.

Foreword

Certain past events stand out as pivotal, as having effects and outcomes that change the course of history. These events are often referred to as turning points. Historian Louis L. Snyder provides this useful definition:

> A turning point in history is an event, happening, or stage which thrusts the course of historical development into a different direction. By definition a turning point is a great event, but it is even more—a great event with the explosive impact of altering the trend of man's life on the planet.

History's turning points have taken many forms. Some were single, brief, and shattering events with immediate and obvious impact. The invasion of Britain by William the Conqueror in 1066, for example, swiftly transformed that land's political and social institutions and paved the way for the rise of the modern English nation. By contrast, other single events were deemed of minor significance when they occurred, only later recognized as turning points. The assassination of a little-known European nobleman, Archduke Franz Ferdinand, on June 28, 1914, in the Bosnian town of Sarajevo was such an event; only after it touched off a chain reaction of political-military crises that escalated into the global conflict known as World War I did the murder's true significance become evident.

Other crucial turning points occurred not in terms of a few hours, days, months, or even years, but instead as evolutionary developments spanning decades or even centuries. One of the most pivotal turning points in human history, for instance—the development of agriculture, which replaced nomadic hunter-gatherer societies with more permanent settlements—occurred over the course of many generations. Still other great turning points were neither events nor developments, but rather revolutionary new inventions and innovations that significantly altered social customs and ideas, military tactics, home life, the spread of knowledge, and the human condition in general. The developments of writing, gunpowder, the printing press, antibiotics, the electric light, atomic energy, television, and the computer, the last two of which have recently ushered in the world-altering information age, represent only some of these innovative turning points.

Each anthology in the Greenhaven Turning Points in World History series presents a group of essays chosen for their accessibility. The anthology's structure also enhances this accessibility. First, an introductory essay provides a general overview of the principal events and figures involved, placing the topic in its historical context. The essays that follow explore various aspects in more detail, some targeting political trends and consequences, others social, literary, cultural, and/or technological ramifications, and still others pivotal leaders and other influential figures. To aid the reader in choosing the material of immediate interest or need, each essay is introduced by a concise summary of the contributing writer's main themes and insights.

In addition, each volume contains extensive research tools, including a collection of excerpts from primary source documents pertaining to the historical events and figures under discussion. In the anthology on the French Revolution, for example, readers can examine the works of Rousseau, Voltaire, and other writers and thinkers whose championing of human rights helped fuel the French people's growing desire for liberty; the French *Declaration of the Rights of Man and Citizen*, presented to King Louis XVI by the French National Assembly on October 2, 1789; and eyewitness accounts of the attack on the royal palace and the horrors of the Reign of Terror. To guide students interested in pursuing further research on the subject, each volume features an extensive bibliography, which for easy access has been divided into separate sections by topic. Finally, a comprehensive index allows readers to scan and locate content efficiently. Each of the anthologies in the Greenhaven Turning Points in World History series provides students with a complete, detailed, and enlightening examination of a crucial historical watershed.

A Brief History of
Early Christianity

The popular modern historian Michael Grant once re-
marked that the appearance and spread of early Christianity
constituted "one of the few revolutions in the world's history
that has lasted."[1] Indeed, that revolution, having political
and social as well as spiritual consequences, has profoundly
affected the evolution and fortunes of many nations, societies and individuals. Since its foundation some two thousand years ago, Christianity has grown into the world's
largest faith, with dozens of denominations and adherents
numbering almost 2 billion. Therefore, the early rise of the
Christian religion, from its humble beginnings in Palestine
in the first century A.D. to its triumph as the dominant faith
of Europe in the early Middle Ages, can justifiably be described as one of history's greatest turning points.

Greco-Roman Influences

The peculiar time and place of Christianity's emergence
profoundly affected the development of Christian ideas and
practices and the manner in which the faith grew and eventually triumphed. Specifically, the social, political, and religious setting of its birth consisted of a mixture of Greco-
Roman and Jewish influences. In the first century, most of
the Mediterranean world was controlled by the Roman Empire, the huge realm that then incorporated lands stretching
from Spain in the west to Palestine in the east, and from
northern Africa in the south to northern Gaul (what are now
France and Belgium) in the north. The Romans gained control of Palestine (the area now occupied by the State of Israel) in the first century B.C. The southern section of Palestine was known as Judaea, an area that had once been the site
of the ancient Jewish kingdom of Judah (destroyed by the
Babylonians in the sixth century B.C.) In A.D. 6, Judaea became an official province of the Roman Empire, with a pre-

fect (later a procurator, also a kind of governor) in charge.

Rome's seizure of Palestine and many other Mediterranean lands created a great deal of social disruption and insecurity among the local peoples of these lands. Disorder and discontent invited the spread of new religions that provided fellowship and hope or promised salvation. Millions of people "were hungry for a faith which would bring them self-respect," states the distinguished historian Kenneth Latourette:

> They sought sustaining companionship, many of them in fellowships which combined religious and social purposes. Longing for the assurance of personal immortality was widespread and reached out wistfully for satisfaction through religious faith and ceremonial.[2]

Not surprisingly, then, many faiths and philosophical schools flourished in the first-, second-, and third-century Roman world; born into that world, Christianity competed with other religions old and new, and as a result grew very slowly, although steadily, in its first three centuries.

Christians generally rejected the teachings of rival faiths during these developmental years. As monotheists, or believers in a single god, they especially shunned the multiple gods of Rome's traditional state religion, including such well-known deities as Jupiter, Juno, Mars, Minerva, and Apollo. Christians also rejected out of hand the existence of the many small personal and household spirits worshiped by most Romans (among them the *lares*, who were thought to keep the house safe, and the *manes*, spirits of deceased ancestors). Yet the early Christians sometimes incorporated some of the ideas and rituals of rival faiths, so Christianity was shaped, at least in part, by currents within the Greco-Roman philosophical and spiritual melting pot.

The Mystery Religions

Particularly popular in this melting pot were several eastern "mystery" cults imported into the Roman world during the last two centuries B.C.[3] The oldest and most widely accepted of these was that of Cybele, the "Great Mother," from Asia Minor, a nature and fertility goddess whose priests castrated themselves to appease her. Her striking initiation rite involved placing the initiate in a pit under a grid; on the grid the priests sacrificed a bull, allowing its blood to drench the person below, who was thereby "reborn" as a member of the faith. Other important mystery cults centered around Mithras, from Persia, whose followers preached treating all people with kindness and respect; and Isis, an Egyptian deity whom the Romans associated with goodness and purification of sin. The second-century A.D. Roman novelist Apuleius provided this description of some of Isis's followers during one of their lavish spring festivals:

> Crowds of those initiated into the divine rites came surging along, men and women of every rank and age, gleaming with linen garments spotlessly white. The women had sprayed their hair with perfume, and covered it with . . . veils; the men had shaved their heads completely, so that their bald pates shone. With their rattles of bronze, silver, and even gold, they made a shrill, tinkling sound. . . . Their leader held out a lamp gleaming with brilliant light. . . . It was a golden boat-shaped vessel feeding quite a large flame from an opening at its center.[4]

Christianity, itself an eastern cult born in Palestine, had many elements in common with the mystery cults. Like Mithraism, for example, it featured the miraculous birth of a sacred baby, a sacramental meal of bread and water (or wine), baptism, and the promise of resurrection. Also, explains classical scholar Charles Freeman:

> Much of the imagery of the New Testament—light and darkness, faith compared to flourishing crops—is similar to that found in mystery religions. The "facts" of Jesus's life were presented in a format which was not unique to him. . . . The promise of an afterlife for the initiated would have been commonplace to anyone who had contact with mystery religions. The development of the cult of Mary, the mother of Jesus, acquires a new richness when placed in parallel with the worship of other mother figures in these religions. . . . Many of the procedures of the mystery religions (initiation

into the cult, for instance) were to act as important influences on Christian practice.[5]

Judaism and Jesus

Of much greater influence on Christianity's inception and development, of course, was the faith from which it sprang—Judaism, the religion of the Jews (hence the later concept of a Judeo-Christian heritage). Christians conceived (and still conceive) their single, all-powerful god as one and the same with the Hebrew god of the Old Testament. The monotheistic Jews had always seen themselves as set apart from other people, both spiritually and culturally; the Christians inherited this feeling of special exclusivity. Moreover, the two faiths shared the same ethical tradition, which emphasized the stability of family life, chastity, and helping the poor and sick. And the Christians carried on many Jewish customs, such as preserving and burying the bodies of the dead (at this time the Romans practiced cremation) and entrusting the spiritual leadership of the community to a council of male elders. Perhaps the most influential of all the carryovers from one faith to the other was the Old Testament (or Scriptures), with its inspiring and enduring stories of the Hebrews' struggles in Egypt, the contributions of prophets like Moses and Isaiah, and the glory days of the ancient kingdoms of Israel and Judah.[6]

For later scholars and theologians, the traditional starting point for the separation of Christianity from Judaism was long seen as the advent of the life and teachings of Jesus Christ.[7] The Jewish society into which Jesus was born was both fragmented and tense. There were conservative groups, such as the Pharisees, who stressed rigid adherence to Jewish Scriptures and law, and the Sadducees, the wealthy and aristocratic Jewish elite, who were prepared to cooperate with the Romans in order to perpetuate their privileged status. And there were more radical groups, notably the Zealots, who urged armed rebellion against the Romans. A delicate political balance existed among these groups, each of which felt it knew what was best for all Jews; any popular leader who threatened the status quo was bound to be seen as a troublemaker by both Jewish and Roman authorities.

It was not Jesus' messages of love and of charity for society's poor and downtrodden that ran him afoul of these authorities; nor was it his prediction that the Kingdom of God, a utopian age of divine rule and eternal salvation, was imminent. These concepts had often been advocated by Jewish holy men of various persuasions, including John the Baptist, the itinerant preacher who baptized Jesus. What made Jesus different was his suggestion that God's new kingdom was not just imminent, but had already begun to arrive on earth, specifically through his own ministry and actions. This seemed to intimate, as many of his followers came to believe, that he was the Messiah, a superhuman figure that Jewish tradition had long prophesied would come to rescue the Jews from centuries-long oppression. Some of Jesus' followers also believed that he was the Son of God. Considering such suggestions and beliefs presumptuous, subversive, and potentially dangerous, the authorities arrested Jesus in about the year A.D. 30 and handed him over to the local Roman prefect, Pontius Pilate. Pilate convicted him of sedition and ordered him to be crucified, a common mode of execution at the time.[8]

The Dead Sea Scrolls and the Qumran Community

It is possible, however, that Jesus' ministry constituted the continuation, rather than beginning, of the split between Judaism and Christianity. The Dead Sea Scrolls, discovered in several remote caves in northern Palestine beginning in 1947, are widely believed by scholars to be the writings of another Jewish sect, the Essenes. The Essenes rejected the life of the Jewish community and retreated to small desert communities, possibly including Qumran, a settlement adjoining one of the Scroll caves. There, they led a strict, monastic existence and waited for the Messiah to usher in the new age.

The many parallels between Essene teachings and beliefs and those of Jesus, along with the fact that many of the Scrolls have been dated to one or two centuries before his birth, have led many scholars to speculate that Jesus was strongly influenced by Essene doctrines. Although no evidence has been found to support the contention that Jesus was himself an Essene, a number of scholars think that John the Baptist may have been a resident of Qumran or some other Essene community. John's preaching and monklike trappings were, after all, strikingly similar to those of the faithful described in the Scrolls. Other scholars see no direct connection between Jesus and the Qumran community and its beliefs. While the controversy continues, James Vanderkam, one of the leading experts on the Scrolls, takes this moderate, somewhat cautious, but realistic stance:

> Clearly, the Qumran literature and the New Testament are similar to one another in numerous and diverse ways. From the similarities, two conclusions can be drawn: (1) The early [Christian] Church grew upon Jewish soil to a far greater extent than previously supposed; and (2) a larger number of the early Church's beliefs and practices than previously suspected were not unique to it.[9]

Paul and the Mission

To whatever degree Jesus may have been influenced by the Jewish spiritual and, especially, apocalyptic ideas and traditions of his day, his own approach to and dissemination of these ideas was unique and powerful enough to cause his death and martyrdom. According to Christian tradition, he rose from the dead and visited with some of his followers (the disciples, or apostles), who then began to spread the word that Jesus was the Messiah and Son of God. Their message was at first directed strictly to Jews, of course, for Jesus' followers still considered themselves Jews and followed Jewish customs, such as circumcision and strict dietary laws. For a while, the new community, calling itself the people of "the Way," consisted of no more than one or two hundred members. They were hated and persecuted by most other Jews and it is possible that, had their ministry remained exclusively Jewish, Christianity might never have grown and triumphed.

In about the year 36, however, an event occurred that virtually assured that growth and triumph. This was the conversion to "the Way" of Saul of Tarsus, later called Paul. Paul was a Jew who at first persecuted the followers of Jesus; but then, according to the account in the New Testament,

> as he . . . approached Damascus . . . suddenly a light from heaven flashed about him. And he fell to the ground and heard a voice saying to him, "Saul, Saul, why do you persecute me?" And he said, "Who are you, Lord?" And he said, "I am Jesus, whom you are persecuting; but rise and enter the city, and you will be told what to do."[10]

In time Paul made it his mission to bring word of Jesus' divinity to the gentiles, or non-Jews, which opened up whole new vistas for attracting converts. As might be expected, most gentiles did not relish the idea of joining a Jewish sect that required them to circumcise themselves and follow Jewish religious laws. So Paul saw the necessity and wisdom of dropping these requirements for gentiles and reached an agreement to that effect with church elders in Jerusalem in about 49.[11] For some time afterward, the Jewish members of the community, which by now called itself Christian,[12] flourished alongside their gentile counterparts, until the former were largely wiped out during the sack of Jerusalem by the Romans in 70.

Having largely separated from Judaism proper, while retaining many Jewish customs, beliefs, and writings, the gentile Christian community began to expand across the Mediterranean world. After the deaths of Paul and the last few original apostles, new generations of missionary leaders took their places. Those of the first century of expansion are often referred to as the Apostolic Fathers, who sought not only to win over new members but also to maintain harmony and set standards of worship among the many far-flung Christian communities. Ignatius of Antioch, for example, wrote letters to various churches advocating that unity could be maintained by rooting out those who denied that Jesus was both human and divine. "There is one physician," he stated circa 112, "fleshly and spiritual, begotten and unbegotten, God in man, true life in death, both of Mary [Jesus' mother] and of God, first passible [capable of suffering] then impassible, Jesus Christ our Lord."[13] Ignatius and other church fathers also stressed the importance of a hierarchy of authority within church organization. In addition to elders, or presbyters (from the Greek word *presbuteros*, meaning "old man"), they said, each community should have a strong overall leader. This was the origin of the office of bishop (from the Greek word *episkopos*, meaning "overseer").

Suspicion and Persecution

In the next few generations, church fathers who came to be known as the apologists were prominent. Among the most famous and influential apologists were Justin (ca. 100–165), Tertullian (ca. 160–240), and Origen (184–254). Generally more educated and worldly than earlier church leaders, the apologists wrote long, persuasive tracts explaining Christian beliefs and calling for toleration and recognition for Christians within Roman society, which was still predominantly pagan, or non-Christian. Justin, for instance, addressed apologies to the emperor Antoninus Pius (reigned 138–161) and the future emperor Marcus Aurelius (Antoninus's adopted son). These writings attempted to answer certain serious charges leveled against Christianity, as well as to show that Christians were loyal to Rome.

It might seem odd that Christianity, which shared so many features with other widely popular faiths of the day, had to defend its very existence so strenuously and for so long among Roman pagans. After all, the Romans were uniquely generous in religious tolerance, as evidenced by the Empire's broad proliferation of gods and beliefs. Out of a sense of patriotism and shared tradition, people of all faiths paid at least occasional homage to the state gods and also to the emperor, whom for political reasons the state represented as semidivine. And members of one faith almost always showed respect for the gods of other faiths. Indeed, belief in syncretism, the idea that all human gods are varied conceptions of one all-powerful god, was common. To an average Roman, worshiping a certain preferred god or gods did not suggest that all other gods were false or inferior; and most people matter-of-factly accepted the notion that there were many diverse paths to the same heavenly truths.

Yet for generations, most Romans viewed the Christians with suspicion, hatred, and even disgust. Historian Harold Mattingly lists some of what were, given the circumstances at the time, quite understandable reasons:

> They [the Christians] refused to worship the [state] gods, insisting on the supremacy of one god of their own; at the same time they paid extraordinary honor to their founder, who had actually been crucified as a dangerous agitator by the Roman governor of Judaea. They were inclined to abstain from the good things of life—from theaters, banquets, shows of amphitheater and circus. More than this, they were suspected of horrible crimes—child murder, incest . . . suspicions that perhaps arose out of genuine misunderstanding of . . . Christian [rituals].[14]

For these reasons, over time the Christians acquired the terrible stigma of having *odium generis humani*, a "hatred for the human race."[15] Worst of all, at least from the state's viewpoint, they would not take part in emperor worship, a refusal viewed by Roman officials as a potential threat to public order. Because the Christians were an antisocial, criminal element that posed a threat to society, went the conventional reasoning, they needed to be restrained and punished before they seriously harmed the community. This was, more or less, the rationale for the series of persecutions the Roman government carried out against them in the first three centuries A.D.

The first such persecution occurred under the emperor Nero (reigned 51–68), who accused the Christians of setting fire to Rome. "During his reign," wrote the second-century Roman historian Suetonius, "a great many public abuses were suppressed by the imposition of heavy penalties. . . . Punishments were also inflicted on the Christians, a sect professing a new and mischievous religious belief."[16] In spite of the efforts of the Christian apologists, other persecutions followed over a course of centuries. The worst was largely instigated by the emperor Galerius in 303, when the government ordered the closing of all Christian churches, the surrender and burning of holy books, and the banning of Christian religious meetings. Other edicts followed and along with them much bloodshed and misery, mainly in the eastern half of the Empire.[17] The fourth-century Christian writer Eusebius recounted some of the horrors:

> We saw with our very eyes the houses of prayer cast down to their foundations . . . and the inspired and sacred Scriptures committed to the flames in the midst of the marketplaces. . . . The spectacle of what followed surpasses all description; for in every place a countless number were shut up, and everywhere the prisons, that long ago had been prepared for murderers and grave robbers, were then filled with [Christians] . . . so that there was no longer any room left for [real criminals].[18]

Constantine the Great

Terrible as it was, the so-called great persecution was the last the Christians had to endure. Fortunately, soon afterward they came under the protective wing of one of the most dynamic, industrious, and tolerant of all Roman emperors—Constantine I, later called the Great. He and his father, Constantius, a coruler with Galerius, had refused to take part in the persecution, and this stance had won Constantine the friendship of several Christian leaders. It appears that in time Constantine also came to see the Christian god as a manifestation of his own favorite god, the Unconquered Sun, the deity worshiped by another of the eastern mystery cults that had become popular in Rome.

This association turned out to be opportune for both himself and the Christians. In 312, at the climax of a bloody power struggle that had rocked the Empire for six years, Constantine marched his army into Italy with the goal of unseating Maxentius, a rival who had illegally declared himself emperor and seized the city of Rome. Ordering his soldiers to paint on their shields a Christian symbol, composed of chi and rho, the first two letters of the Greek version of Christ's name, Constantine proceeded to annihilate his opponent's forces.[19] The next day, October 29, 312, Constantine entered

Rome in triumph, proudly displaying on his helmet the chi-rho sign, which he used as his battle token from then on.

Clearly, Constantine was convinced that the Christian god had ensured his victory and he was now willing and eager to reward both that deity and its followers. During his ensuing reign, therefore, Christianity underwent a relatively sudden transition from a minor, misunderstood, often hated and persecuted faith, to a widely tolerated, legally sanctioned, and rapidly growing one. Toleration came only a year after Constantine's victory, which made him undisputed ruler of the western sector of the Empire. In February 313, at Milan, in northern Italy, he met with Licinius, who claimed sovereignty over the east; shortly afterward Licinius issued in both their names what became known as the Edict of Milan, granting official toleration to Christians throughout the Empire. The document began:

> When under happy auspices I, Constantine Augustus, and I, Licinius Augustus, had come to Milan and held an inquiry about all matters such as pertain to the common advantage and good . . . we resolved to issue decrees by which esteem and reverence for the Deity might be procured, that is, that we might give all Christians freedom of choice to follow the ritual which they wished.[20]

Constantine's support for the Christians remained steadfast in the later years of his reign. His chief role in church affairs in this period was as mediator of several serious disputes that arose among the bishops, whom he recognized as the faith's political as well as spiritual leaders. The first major dispute arose in 313, when a group of church leaders, who became known as the Donatists, heatedly argued that those Christians who had caved in and surrendered the Scriptures during the great persecution were impure and immoral. The influential bishop of Rome denounced the Donatists, as did most other bishops; Constantine took the same position, ordering in 316 that Donatists be expelled from their churches.

Much more serious and far-reaching was the controversy that arose a decade later, known as the Arian heresy, after Arius, a priest of Alexandria, Egypt. Arius claimed that Jesus was not one and the same with God, but rather a separate being who was posterior, or inferior, to the Creator. Arianism caused such a stir among church leaders that Constantine felt compelled to intervene. He called a great council of bishops in 325 at Nicaea, in Asia Minor, where he sided with the majority against the Arians. He appears to have suggested that the church adopt the concept of *homoousios*, "of the same substance," essentially meaning that Christ and God were one and the same.

Another great service Constantine performed for Christianity was his founding of Constantinople, "the city of Constantine," (on the Bosporus strait, separating Europe from Asia) on May 11, 330. He dedicated the city to the Virgin Mary and Holy Trinity; and over the years it grew into a mighty Christian bastion that managed to survive the later fall of the western Empire. Constantine also poured vast sums of money into church-building programs. "All over the Empire new churches appeared," writes Freeman,

> resplendent with their fine decoration. . . . Many were built over the shrines of martyrs, places which had been venerated since the early days of the church. Others took over prime sites within the major cities—even the sites of earlier imperial palaces. . . . Churches now became magnificent treasure houses, objects of awe and inspiration of worship. . . . [For their design] there was a pagan model to copy: the basilica, typically a long hall with a flat timber roof and aisles running along its length. For centuries the basilicas had been used as law courts . . . or [as] places to meet and gossip. Now they were to receive a new function. . . . The greatest of the basilicas was St. Peter's in Rome, constructed over the shrine which for generations was believed to be the resting place of St. Peter's [one of the Twelve Apostles] body.[21]

The Onrushing Christian Tide

Thanks in large degree to Constantine's pro-Christian policies, after his death Christianity underwent spectacular growth, gaining political as well as spiritual authority. His three sons—Constantine II, Constantius II, and Constans—

were all pious and committed Christians. Their successor, Julian (reigned 361–363), attempted to strengthen the status of the declining pagan faiths in an effort to stem the on-rushing Christian tide, but he died in battle before he could effect any lasting change and proved to be the Empire's last pagan emperor. Under his successors, paganism found itself increasingly under attack by zealous Christian bishops.

The most prominent and influential of these bishops was Ambrose of Milan (ca. 340–397). He convinced the emperor Gratian (ruled in the west 367–383) to give up the post of *pontifex maximus*, chief priest of the state religion (tradition-ally held by the emperors). Urged on by Ambrose, Gratian also confiscated the funds of the state priesthood and re-moved the time-honored altar of the goddess Victory from the Senate.

At the same time, Ambrose and other bishops vehemently attacked paganism. One of their most common themes was that God had placed the Roman Empire on earth as a "seedbed" for Christianity; therefore, it mattered little whether Rome survived, as long as humanity embraced God. Pagan writers responded by defending Rome and its tradi-tional values. In a famous heated exchange between Am-brose and an influential senator named Symmachus, the lat-ter called for understanding and tolerance on both sides: "What difference does it make by what pains each seeks the truth? We cannot attain to so great a secret by one road."[22] But Christian leaders increasingly recognized their own road as the only route to heavenly truths, as demonstrated by Ambrose's uncompromising reply: "You worship the works of your own hands; we think it an offense that anything which can be made should be esteemed God."[23] The next emperor to come under Ambrose's persuasive influence was Theodosius I (ruled in the east 379–392; east and west 392–395), who abolished all pagan sacrifices and cults and officially closed all pagan temples.[24] Thus, although the number of pagans in the Empire remained large, by the 390s Christian leaders had managed to achieve a controlling in-fluence over the political and religious apparatus of the Roman state.

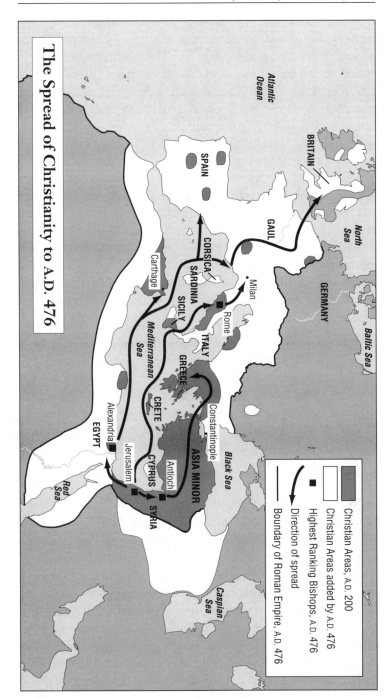

The Spread of Christianity to A.D. 476

Christian Areas, A.D. 200

Christian Areas added by A.D. 476

Highest Ranking Bishops, A.D. 476

Direction of spread

Boundary of Roman Empire, A.D. 476

In the next two generations, other Christian leaders and writers continued to carry the Christian revolution into Roman social and personal life. The church labeled such pastimes as gambling, gladiatorial combats, horse racing, and mixed public bathing as sinful. Female virginity became a treasured virtue; and sexual activity, outside of married couples attempting to create children, was increasingly frowned on.

Meanwhile, a growing number of Christians decided that the best way to venerate God was not to change society, but rather to withdraw from it. In the mid-to-late fourth century and on into the fifth, thousands of people chose a secluded, monklike existence in remote retreats not unlike that of the Jews of Qumran. This was the beginning of the monastic movement that would become a major and accepted feature of medieval Christian life; at its inception, however, as noted scholar Henry Chadwick remarks, it was controversial:

> The complex motives that drove men and women to become hermits or, more commonly, to join communities of ascetics living under obedience are only partly visible to us. The fourth-century Church experienced the movement as a shock to its system. Many bishops opposed the weakening of urban or village congregations which resulted from the exodus of the most dedicated members into special separate communities owing an allegiance to their abbot and often showing a cool reserve to the ordinary life of the Church.[25]

Spiritual Guide for Europe

The growing monastic movement was only an extreme example of the way in which Christian thought was changing both society as a whole and the moral outlook of individuals. For instance, under the influence of late Roman Christian writers, perhaps the most influential among them Augustine (354–430), intense guilt and the fear of eternity in hell began to replace public shame as conditioners of moral behavior. Some earlier Christian thinkers, notably Origen, had argued that God was too good and compassionate to condemn people to such a terrible place as hell. But Augustine rejected this view and warned that sin would lead to eternal punishment. Augustine also strongly advocated the doctrine of original sin, the idea that Adam and Eve's transgressions in the Garden of Eden had condemned all people to begin life as sinners. Only by gaining God's grace through the sacrament of baptism, said Augustine, could a person be accepted into heaven.

Augustine is second only to Paul as a shaper of Christian thought. His writings, including the monumental *City of God*, in which he criticized Greco-Roman culture and showed how God's purpose was revealed in the fabric of prior historical events, exerted a profound influence on medieval and early modern thinkers and theologians. One of the themes of Augustine's *City of God* is that God's true city was the growing brotherhood of Christian believers, which extended in the spiritual sense from earth into heaven. The earthly, more material city of Rome, he said, was transient and ultimately unimportant in the grand scheme of things; so it mattered little whether Rome passed away as long as the heavenly city survived.

This concept of Christianity surviving the passing of Rome proved prophetic. Only a generation after Augustine's death, the western Empire, already crippled and shrunken from years of poor leadership, economic decline, and attacks by so-called barbarians from northern Europe, collapsed. Eastern Rome survived in the form of the Byzantine Empire, but over the centuries the East increasingly went its own way. In the West, the church survived the fall of Rome and now set about converting those barbarians who had not already accepted Christian beliefs.

At the forefront of the effort to Christianize Europe were missionaries sent by church leaders, one of the most influential being Pope Gregory I (540–604). "Coming on the scene at the time of widespread political confusion," explains Kings College scholar Howard Vos,

> he became a stabilizing political influence and was largely responsible for the creation of the medieval papacy. . . . Gregory's great achievement was to organize the papal govern-

ment as an elaborate, smoothly functioning machine in a period when society in Italy and the West in general was falling irretrievably into decay. . . . He transformed the bishopric of Rome into a papal system that endured through the Middle Ages.[26]

Gregory also sent forty monks to England in about 596, a mission that led to the foundation of the Church of England, with its spiritual capital at Canterbury, one of the great Christian bastions of later Europe. As Christian conversions spread like a chain reaction across the continent, many other such bastions arose; in succeeding centuries, Christianity, having risen to the position of spiritual guide for all of Europe, reached out to embrace minds and hearts across the globe. Truly, Paul's humble mission, which began with his own conversion outside ancient Damascus, initiated one of the great success stories of history.

Notes

1. Michael Grant, *History of Rome*. New York: Scribner's, 1978. Reprint: History Book Club, 1997, p. 342.

2. Kenneth S. Latourette, *A History of Christianity*. New York: Harper and Brothers, 1953, p. 22.

3. The term "mystery" referred to the fact that these cults invariably featured secret initiations usually known only to fellow members; many of the rituals of these cults were modeled on or at least similar to those of the cults of Demeter, goddess of plants, and the fertility god Dionysus, both worshiped in early Greece.

4. Apuleius, *The Golden Ass* 11.10. Trans. P.G. Walsh. New York: Oxford University Press, 1995, p. 224.

5. Charles Freeman, *Egypt, Greece, and Rome*. New York: Oxford University Press, 1996, p. 490.

6. Jews call the first five books of the Old Testament (Genesis, Exodus, Leviticus, Numbers, and Deuteronomy) the Torah; Christians call it the Pentateuch.

7. His given name was Jesus; the name Christ came from the Greek word *Christos*, meaning messiah, or anointed one, and was used by his followers only after his death.

8. The charge of sedition was based on Jesus' refusal to deny that he was the "king of the Jews," which, in Roman eyes, implied that he might pose a threat to Rome's imperial throne.

9. James Vanderkam, "The Dead Sea Scrolls and Christianity," in Hershel Shanks, ed., *Understanding the Dead Sea Scrolls*. New York: Random House, 1992, p. 201. The possible connections among Jesus, the Essenes, and the Qumran writings are not the only controversies surrounding the Dead Sea Scrolls. Some scholars charge that an elite, arrogant group of biblical experts

held a shameful monopoly over access to many of the Scrolls until all were released publicly in the late 1980s; others claim that the Catholic Church long tried to suppress the contents of some of the more controversial scrolls; see Michael Baigent and Richard Leigh, *The Dead Sea Scrolls Deception*. New York: Summit Books, 1991; the introduction to Robert Eisenman and Michael Wise, *The Dead Sea Scrolls Uncovered*. New York: Penguin Books, 1992; and "Is the Vatican Suppressing the Dead Sea Scrolls?" in Shanks, *Understanding the Dead Sea Scrolls*, pp. 275–90.

10. Acts 9.3–6, Holy Bible, Revised Standard Version. New York: Thomas Nelson and Sons, 1952.

11. Most of the elders were reluctant and ruled that though gentiles could forgo circumcision and some other Jewish customs, they had to conform to Jewish moral standards.

12. According to Acts 11.26, the term "Christian" was coined by the members of "the Way" living in Antioch, Syria (north of Palestine).

13. *Incarnation*, quoted in Henry Bettenson, ed., *Documents of the Christian Church*. London: Oxford University Press, 1967, p. 29.

14. Harold Mattingly, *The Man in the Roman Street*. New York: W.W. Norton, 1966, p. 56.

15. The phrase comes from the *Annals* (15.43) of the first-century Roman historian Tacitus, who cites it as one of the reasons (the other being arson) for the arrest of many Christians following the great fire that devastated Rome in A.D. 64. Tacitus either coined the phrase or repeated one that had already become common.

16. *Nero* 16, in *Lives of the Twelve Caesars*, published as *Suetonius: The Twelve Caesars*, trans. Robert Graves, rev. Michael Grant. New York: Penguin Books, 1979, p. 221.

17. At the time, the administration of the Roman realm was divided among four sovereigns (the Tetrarchy), two of whom (Diocletian and Galerius) ruled Rome's eastern sphere from Asia Minor (what is now Turkey), while the others (Maximian and Constantius) ruled the western sphere from Gaul.

18. *Ecclesiastical History*, quoted in Naphtali Lewis and Meyer Reinhold, eds., *Roman Civilization, Sourcebook 2: The Empire*. New York: Harper and Row, 1966, pp. 599–600.

19. The day before, Constantine had supposedly seen a celestial vision—a cross of light bearing the inscription "Conquer by This." Since the story was recorded many years later by Eusebius, a Christian writer attempting to glorify both Constantine and the Christian god and to strengthen the connection between them, it may be a fabrication. If, on the other hand, Constantine did see a cross in the sky, it may have been a rare phenomenon called a solar halo, caused by sunlight reflecting on ice crystals in the upper atmosphere. For a more detailed discussion, see A.H.M. Jones, *Constantine and the Conversion of Europe*. Toronto: University of Toronto Press, 1978, pp. 85–86.

20. Quoted in Eusebius, *Ecclesiastical History*, 2 vols. trans. Roy J. Deferrari. Washington, DC: Catholic University of America Press, 1955, vol. 1, p. 269.

21. Charles Freeman, *The World of the Romans*. New York: Oxford University Press, 1993, pp.162-63.

22. *On the Altar of Victory*, quoted in Brian Tierney, ed., *The Middle Ages, vol. 1, Sources of Medieval History*. New York: Knopf, 1973, p. 24.

23. *Letter to Valentinian II*, quoted in Tierney, *Sources of Medieval History*, p. 26.

24. Some temples were demolished, some turned into museums, and others transformed into Christian churches.

25. "Envoi: On Taking Leave of Antiquity," in John Boardman et al., eds., *The Oxford History of the Roman World*. New York: Oxford University Press, 1988, pp. 469–70.

26. Howard F. Vos, *Introduction to Church History*. Nashville: Thomas Nelson and Sons, 1994, pp. 88–89.

Chapter 1

The Birth of Christianity

Turning | Points
IN WORLD HISTORY

The Jewish Background of Christianity

John G. Davies

John G. Davies, a former professor of theology at the University of Birmingham and highly regarded authority on early Christianity, explains the ancient Jewish traditions, writings, and ideas that shaped the thinking of the various Jewish sects of Jesus' day and profoundly influenced Jesus' own thinking as well as that of John the Baptist, the preacher who baptized him.

The origins of Christianity go back to the activities of a Palestinian Jew, by the name of Jesus, who was born in the reign of Herod the Great and conducted his mission under Pontius Pilate, the Roman procurator from AD 26–36. Since Jesus was a Jew and his relations were mainly, though not exclusively, with those of his own race, if he is to be set firmly within his historical context something must be said of the Judaism in which he was nurtured and grew up. Like any other Jew of the period, Jesus cannot but have been conscious of his nation's past and have shared with his contemporaries their hopes and aspirations which were based upon that past. Its record was contained in their sacred writings, which were divided into three sections: the Law, being the Pentateuch or first five books of the Old Testament; the prophets, consisting of the Former, i.e. Joshua, Judges, I and II Samuel, and I and II Kings, and the Latter, i.e. the major and minor prophets, and the writings, i.e. Psalms, Proverbs, Song of Songs, Ruth, Lamentations, Ecclesiastes, Esther, Daniel, Ezra, Nehemiah and I and II Chronicles.

Excerpted from J.G. Davies, *The Early Christian Church* (New York: Holt, Rinehart & Winston, 1965).

From these holy books the Jew learned of God's dealings with Israel from the time when the twelve tribes were united under Moses to form a nation. This story was set within a universal context by the opening chapters of Genesis which tell how God created heaven and earth and man in his own image. Then followed man's rebellion against God and his consequent corruption. The divine method of coping with this situation was to select one individual, Abraham, out of the fallen mass of mankind that his descendants might be taught the will of God and be the medium whereby all nations could be brought back to serve their Creator.

The Jewish Covenant with God

It was these descendants who were delivered by God from bondage in Egypt and were united to him by a covenant ratified on Mount Sinai. The Terms of this agreement were specified in the law promulgated through Moses, and henceforth the Jews were the chosen people of God, elected not to privilege but to service as the agents of his purpose. So they were brought into the Promised Land and given a king as the divine representative, and with him too God entered into a covenant, which however contained no stipulation but rested on the firm promise: 'thy throne shall be established for ever'. Now began that period which to the Jew of Jesus' day was the Golden Age of Israelite history—the age of the shepherd king, David, the Lord's Messiah or Anointed One, the age of his son Solomon, when the kingdom stretched from Kadesh in the north to Eziongeber in the south and when the Temple, the shrine of the Ark and the focus of the divine presence, was built in Jerusalem; the age of freedom, independence and peace. But, so the story continues, the glory soon passed; the one people split into two, organized into the northern and southern kingdoms. . . . The northern kingdom was swept away by the Assyrians under Sennacherib, its capital Samaria falling in 722. Then the southern half . . . came under the rule of the Babylonians led by Nebuchadnezzar, its capital Jerusalem being devastated in 587 and its leading citizens deported.

The experience of the Exile bit deep into the Jewish soul.

It gave him an acute sense of sin, since he accepted the prophetic interpretation of these events as punishment for failure to obey the divine commands, and hence the Day of Atonement became the major religious festival of the year; it gave him abhorrence of all that might contaminate him in his daily life, and hence he sought to separate himself from the non-Jew or Gentile; it gave him an earnest desire to know the divine will and to do it, so as to avoid the repetition of such a calamity, and hence the codification of the law. ... The sacred scriptures were no longer regarded as the historical record of God's dealings with his people; they were a book of divine law. In binding herself to her past, thus understood, Israel loosed her ties with the present; God was not so much the God of history but the God about to come and the chosen people were conceived to be not those with a mission to fulfill but the holy nation, separated from all worldly interests and ideals. . . .

Divergent Parties and Views

The contrast between . . . oppression and suffering and the divine promises contained in the books of the law induced in the Jew a profound pessimism about the present age [i.e., the time of Jesus] and a fervent hope in the intervention of God to bring it to an end, to overthrow the forces of evil and to honour his covenant with the Davidic house. This hope was fostered by the writings of the apocalyptic school, such as the book of Daniel, a genre of literature . . . which described visions of the future, often regarded as imminent, and expressed the certainty of the ultimate triumph of God and the glorification of his people Israel. So a new Golden Age was envisaged, when God's Kingdom or rule would be set up, exercised either directly or through his promised Messiah.

Judaism thus had two poles: the hope of the future and the fulfilment of the law; but it would be a mistake to assume that there was a rigidly uniform attitude to these. Just as the apocalyptists did not agree amongst themselves in presenting an identical blue-print of the expected end, so the Jews as a whole differed in their understanding of the law, and these differences were reflected in the several parties that emerged in the post-exilic period and were distinct and active at the time of Jesus. . . .

One source of divergent views was disagreement as to the extent of the law. The Sadducees, who were in the main the aristocratic priestly party, accepted the authority of the written Torah and refused to countenance any additions to it. The Pharisees, who developed out of the lay scribes, upheld the equal importance of the oral tradition. . . . The Sadducees endorsed the strictest fulfilment of the written law, but challenged the Pharisees' readiness to modify it. The Pharisees asserted the unlimited obligation of the living tradition and opposed the Sadducean political prudence and willingness to co-operate with the authorities of the occupying power, which allowed freedom to Temple worship and the Jewish courts. . . . Both however had a certain common ground in the worship of the Temple and the synagogue. . . . Both too had common ground in their opposition to the Essenes who combined different elements from Sadduceeism and Pharisaism. Thus, like the former, they [the Essenes] were adherents of the traditions of priesthood with their own rites of purification and a sacred meal. . . . Like the latter they practiced a rigorous observance of the law, cherished apocalyptic hopes and claimed to be the true people of God. Unlike either, however, the Essenes formed an ascetic monastic society withdrawn from common life. . . . The Essenes shunned the direct political action which was the policy of the Zealots. These were groups of partisans who stimulated and supported rebellious movements against the occupying power and were characterized by the profession of a theocratic ideal and fervent Messianic hopes. . . .

The Coming of John the Baptist

[In the midst of the political tensions arising out of these divergent views] John appears abruptly on the scene—Luke alone provides some information about his childhood. John is dressed in the traditional garb of a prophet, with a leather girdle around his loins, like [the prophet] Elijah of old. Here is a new note in post-exilic Judaism; the divine moratorium on prophecy has come to an end, since a genuine prophet, accepted as such by the crowds that flock to him, has now appeared. This could have only one meaning: the decisive action of God was imminent. This indeed was the burden of the Baptist's message: 'Who warned you to flee from the wrath to come? . . . And even now is the axe also laid unto the root of the trees: every tree therefore that bringeth not forth good fruit is hewn down, and cast into the fire'. John thus stood in the line of the Old Testament prophets and his message was a solemn warning of judgement to come, coupled with a call to repentance. Its difference lay in the stress on the urgent nearness of the time of God's Kingdom. John himself prepared his hearers for this coming by administering a baptism in water. . . . This baptism was a prophetic sign . . . a guarantee, more than a mere promise, that those who were sealed in this way would pass safely through the impending tribulation and secure a place in the Kingdom.

John also specified the agent of this impending judgement: 'there cometh he that is mightier than I, the latchet of whose shoes I am not worthy to unloose . . . whose fan is in his hand, throughly to cleanse his threshing-floor, and to gather the wheat into his garner; but the chaff he will burn up with unquenchable fire'. Here is no fulfiller of political aspirations, but the judge of the world who brings a baptism of fire. According to the Christian tradition this person is none other than Jesus of Nazareth.

Christianity in the World of Ancient Rome

Kenneth Scott Latourette

The late Kenneth Scott Latourette was a distinguished university professor, historian, president of the American Historical Association, and author of one of the most acclaimed and widely read modern histories of Christianity. This essay, taken from that volume, explores the first-century A.D. Mediterranean setting in which the first small Christian communities grew. As Latourette points out, the new faith was fortunate to begin in that particular time and place. Specifically, it grew during the *Pax Romana*, or "Roman Peace," the roughly two-centuries-long era of unprecedented peace and prosperity that began with Augustus Caesar's acquisition of ultimate power in the early 20s B.C. The political unity, excellent road systems, and safety of trade and travel during this period greatly facilitated the spread of Jesus' teachings.

If Christianity was radically different from Judaism, the religion which in some degree was its parent, the gulf which separated it from the Græco-Roman world into which it was born was still wider. It was an alien environment into which Christianity came.

Yet much in that environment favoured the spread of Christianity. Moreover, the environment placed its stamp on Christianity. We must, therefore, seek to understand something of the main outline of the life and thought of the portion of the globe outside of Judaism in which Christianity

Excerpted from *A History of Christianity*, by Kenneth Scott Latourette. Copyright ©1953 by Harper & Brothers, renewed ©1981 by Wilma E. Hogg, Errol Hollowel, and Alan Hollowel. Revised edition copyright ©1975 by Harper & Row, Publishers, Inc. Reprinted by permission of HarperCollins Publishers, Inc.

had its beginning.

First of all, we must remind ourselves again that the basin of the Mediterranean, the region in which Christianity came into being, in which it had its first great triumphs, and in which it long had most of its strength, embraced only a small fraction of the earth's surface. Moreover, when Christ was born it was the home of considerably less than half of civilized mankind. Culturally it presented a great variety, but in general it was dominated by two traditions, those of Greece and Rome. . . .

Since it had its birth, its first triumphs, and its initial chief stronghold in the Græco-Roman world, Christianity was profoundly moulded by it. In organization and in thought it conformed in part to it. It came to be largely identified with what is called the Occident, that portion of mankind which is the heir of Greece, Roman, and itself. Only occasionally did it spread extensively among non-Occidental peoples. Not until recently has it gained substantial footing in all the other great cultural units and among the majority of the primitive groups of mankind. Only within the past few decades has it become actually world-wide. It still has its main centres in the Occident. While lately it has made tremendous strides towards becoming universal, it has not yet divested itself of the integuments [trappings] which it acquired during its Occidental pilgrimage.

The Blessings of Peace

At the time when Christianity came into being, much in the basin of the Mediterranean favoured the spread of religions, either new or old. Jesus was born in the reign of Augustus. After a long period of wars which had racked the Mediterranean and its shores, political unity had been achieved and the Roman Empire had become roughly coterminous with the Mediterranean Basin. Here and there it was soon to spread beyond it. Augustus was the first Emperor. Building on the foundations laid by his uncle, Julius Caesar, he brought peace and under the guise of the chief citizen of a restored republic ruled the realm which for several generations Rome had been building. The internal peace and order which

Augustus achieved endured, with occasional interruptions, for about two centuries. Never before had all the shores of the Mediterranean been under one rule and never had they enjoyed such prosperity. The *pax Romana* made for the spread of ideas and religions over the area where it prevailed.

With the *pax Romana* went the building of roads and the

Praises for Rome's Achievement

In this excerpt from his famous Roman Panegyric, *the second-century Greek orator Aelius Aristides sings Rome's praises for unifying and bringing culture and order to the Mediterranean world. Without this unity and order, the Christians' task of spreading their beliefs and founding new communities in faraway lands would have been much more difficult.*

Every place is full of gymnasia, fountains, gateways, temples, shops, and schools. . . . Gifts never stop flowing from you to the cities; and because of your impartial generosity to all, the leading beneficiaries cannot be determined. Cities shine in radiance and beauty, and the entire countryside is decked out like a pleasure ground. . . . Festivity, like a holy, unquenchable fire, never fails, but goes around from one place to the next and is always somewhere, for it fits in with the universal prosperity. And so, only those outside your Empire, if there are any, are fit to be pitied for losing such blessings. . . . Greek and barbarian can now readily go wherever they please with their property or without it. It is just like going from their own to their own country. Neither the Cilician Gates nor the narrow, sandy approaches through Arabia to Egypt present any danger. Nor do impassable mountains, vast stretches of river, or inhospitable barbarian tribes. For safety, it is enough to be a Roman, or rather, one of your subjects. . . .

You have surveyed the whole world, built bridges of all sorts across rivers, cut down mountains to make paths for chariots, filled the deserts with hostels, and civilized it all with system and order.

Naphtali Lewis and Meyer Reinhold, eds., *Roman Civilization, Sourcebook 2: The Empire.* New York: Harper and Row, 1966, p. 138.

growth of commerce. Highways of solid construction traversed the Empire and made possible more extensive travel and trade than the region had ever known. The pirates had been curbed who had imperilled shipping in the Mediterranean. Roads, travel, and commerce facilitated cultural and religious as well as political unity.

Travel and trade were accompanied by the spread of two languages, Greek and Latin. Greek was spoken among one or more groups in most of the cities of the Empire where commerce was to be found. The Greek-speaking and Greek-reading groups were most numerous in the eastern part of the Mediterranean. Alexandria in Egypt was a particularly prominent focus of Greek culture. Yet those for whom Greek was a primary tongue were also present in Rome, in Sicily and the south of Italy, in some of the cities of the south of Gaul, and in several other centres in the western portions of the Mediterranean. . . . Latin was more prevalent in the West. In the first centuries of the Christian era, while Christianity was expanding in the Empire, it was increasingly the speech of much of the population on the western borders of the Mediterranean. A religion which employed Greek and Latin, and especially Greek, had advantages over rivals which did not and might gain an Empire-wide hearing.

Religious Melting Pots

Important also was the religious and moral hunger which characterized much of the populace of the basin of the Mediterranean in the centuries in which Christianity was having its early development. The formation of an all-embracing empire promoted the decay of the local religious cults of the several states and cities which were brought within the inclusive political unity. To be sure, many were maintained as a matter of custom or civic pride, but the heart had largely gone out of them. Then, too, the advancing intelligence and moral sensitivity of the times cast doubt upon the stories about the gods. Many of these were both incredible to an educated mind and offensive to the morally sensitive. The gods were not as good as the best men of the period and could command respect only if the stories about them were treated as myths and allegorized. The age had in it much of moral corruption. Yet it also had consciences which revolted against the excesses of the day. A religion which offered high moral standards and the power to attain them would be welcomed by the more serious.

The times brought with them much of insecurity. In the comprehensive political unity many individuals were up-rooted from their accustomed environment and either as slaves, as soldiers, or by free choice found themselves unsupported by the social group in which they had been reared. While in part outwardly preserved and even strengthened, the old city states which had characterized the Mediter-ranean world and which gave their free citizens a sense of community were basically weakened, absorbed in the large impersonal Empire. Millions were disinherited . . . slaves on the great landed estates or in city mansions, many of them from distant parts of the Empire. They were hungry for a faith which would bring them self-respect. They sought sus-taining companionship, many of them in fellowships which combined religious with social purposes. Longing for the as-surance of personal immortality was widespread and reached out wistfully for satisfaction through religious faith and cer-emonial. As cities multiplied and grew in size, made up as many of them were of strangers and their children, and, like the Empire, impersonal, they provided favourable environ-ment for novel religious ideas and for religious fellowships. They were melting pots into which many religions entered.

Searching for a Sense of Safety

When, towards the close of the second century, disasters began to overtake the Roman Empire and society was threatened with progressive disintegration, many turned to religion for the remedy. Augustus and his successors had not solved the basic problems of the Mediterranean world. They had obscured them. For what appeared to be a failure in gov-ernment they had substituted more government, and gov-ernment was not the answer. Confidence in man's ability and reason was shaken. There was a widespread "loss of nerve." Religion was looked to for the sense of safety which had been lost. Moreover, there was a groping towards some kind of theism, towards a unifying principle or deity which could bring cohesion and in the confusion yield an inkling of a universe which would correspond to the political and economic unity which the Roman Empire had brought to the Mediterranean world. Distrusting themselves and their reason, men looked for the answer in antiquity and in religions which could claim the sanctions of the ancients and of long generations of believers.

John the Baptist's Role in the Birth of Christianity

Otto Betz

The Dead Sea Scrolls have remained controversial since the first of these ancient documents were discovered in a Palestine cave in 1947. A good many biblical scholars and classical historians believe that the Scrolls are the writings of the monastic Essene sect and that Essene religious doctrines mark the beginning of the transition from Judaism to Christianity. That view is summarized here by Otto Betz, former professor of the New Testament at Chicago Theological Seminary and a leading Scrolls scholar. Citing the works of the ancient Jewish historian Josephus, various parts of the New Testament, and portions of the Scrolls, Betz makes the case that the Qumran community, near the Dead Sea shore, was an Essene retreat and that John the Baptist was likely influenced by Essene doctrines.

The Dead Sea Scrolls provide us with a picture of a first-century Jewish community that could well have been the home of John the Baptist. At the very least, the possibility is worth exploring. The question is not answered easily, nor is it without difficulty. My own view is that the Baptist was raised in this community by the Dead Sea and was strongly influenced by it, but later left it to preach directly to a wider community of Jews.

Paradoxically, our sources in some ways portray John the Baptist more clearly than Jesus. It is certainly easier to place John in relationship to the contemporaneous Jewish community. Moreover, for John, we have an additional, nonbiblical witness—the first-century Jewish historian Josephus who refers to Jesus but tells little about him. Even among hypercritical exegetes [text interpreters], there is little doubt about who John was and what he stood for.

The Dead Sea Scrolls give us an extraordinary contemporary picture of a Jewish sect, living in the wilderness, with an outlook, customs, and laws that seem to be very much like John's.

Most scholars, including myself, identify the Dead Sea Scroll community as Essene—a separatist Jewish sect or philosophy described, along with the Pharisees and Sadducees, by Josephus.

Recently some few scholars have questioned whether the Dead Sea Scroll community was Essene. They contend that the library of scrolls found in the Dead Sea caves represents broader Jewish thought. However this may be, it is clear that the library's core documents—to which I shall refer—are, at the least, Essenic, and represent the commitment of a Jewish community quite distinct from—even opposed to—the Jerusalem authorities.

Moreover, in the Judean wilderness, archaeologists have identified and excavated a settlement near where the scrolls were found. According to [the Roman naturalist] Pliny the Elder, in *Historia Naturalis*, the Essenes lived in just this location. Indeed, of the eleven caves with inscriptional material, the one with the greatest number of documents—Cave 4—could be entered from the adjacent settlement. . . .

We shall assume that this settlement, which overlooks the Wadi Qumran, was Essene and that the sectarian documents found in the Qumran caves are also Essene.

The Stature of John the Baptist

As portrayed in the Gospels, John the Baptist stands at the threshold of the Kingdom. He marks the transition from Judaism to Christianity.

Not only is the Gospel picture generally consistent with Josephus, but the four canonical Gospels are themselves in general agreement. In the case of John, there is little room for historical skepticism.

The Gospels portray John as a prophet who came out of the Judean wilderness to proclaim the Kingdom of God and to call for repentance. It seems clear that he had a successful ministry of his own, baptizing with water those who repented.

After Herod the Great died in 4 B.C., his son Herod Antipas became tetrarch of Galilee. John denounced Antipas' marriage to Herodias, his half-niece, who had abandoned her previous husband. Antipas threw John into prison for his criticism. Antipas' new wife Herodias, however, was to go one step further. At Antipas' birthday party, Salome, Herodias's daughter by her previous marriage and now Antipas' step-daughter, danced for Antipas, who was so delighted with her performance that he promised on oath to give Salome whatever she desired. Induced by her mother Herodias, Salome asked for the head of John the Baptist on a platter. Antipas was unhappy at the request but was bound by his oath. He had John beheaded in prison, which Josephus locates at the fortress of Machaerus, east of the Jordan, and his head was duly delivered to Salome on a platter (Matthew 14:3–12; Mark 6:17–29).

John's stature is reflected in the fact that when Antipas is informed of Jesus' ministry and wondrous deeds, his first thought is that John had been resurrected and had come back to life (Matthew 14:1–2; Mark 6:14–16; Luke 9:7–9).

The Gospels portray John as the forerunner of Jesus. Jesus himself proclaims John's stature: "Truly, I say to you, among those born of women there has risen no one greater then John the Baptist" (Matthew 11:11; compare Luke 7:28). John, Jesus tells the crowd, is "more than a prophet" (Matthew 11:9; Luke 5:26). Indeed, "he is Elijah to come" (Matthew 11:14), the traditional precursor of the Messiah. Jesus himself was baptized by John (Matthew 3:13–17; Mark 1:9–11; Luke 3:21–22). It is clear that the populace considered John a true prophet (Matthew 21:26; Mark 11:32; Luke 20:6). According to Josephus, John "was a good man and had commanded the Jews to lead a virtuous life.". . .

John the Baptist has been immortalized through innumerable works of art—novels, operas, movies, and especially paintings—showing the prophet preaching in the desert, baptizing in the Jordan River, or pointing to the lamb of God. We see him as a prisoner in a dark cell, or sometimes only his bloody head on a platter being delivered to the beautiful Salome. The Baptist was also a favorite of icon painters. As the *prodromos*, the precursor of Christ, he stands at the left hand of the Judge of the World. . . .

John and Qumran

It is not surprising that the discovery and partial publication of the Dead Sea Scrolls has led to speculation that John the Baptist was an Essene who lived at Qumran. The Essenes flourished at Qumran at the same time John was preaching and baptizing people in the nearby Jordan River. The Qumran settlement was destroyed by the Romans in about 68 A.D. as part of their effort to suppress the First Jewish Revolt against Rome (66 to 70 A.D.), which culminated in the destruction of Jerusalem.

The Dead Sea Scroll known as the Manual of Discipline, also called the Rule of the Community . . . appears to be the main organizational document of the Qumran community. There we read that the people of the community must separate themselves

> from the dwelling-place of the men of perversion [the Jerusalem authorities] in order to go to the wilderness to prepare the way of HIM, as it is written [quoting Isaiah 40:3]: "In the wilderness prepare the way of. . . . [the divine name is marked in this scroll by four dots], make straight in the desert a road for our God!"—this [way] is the search of the Law (Manual of Discipline 8:13–15).

The Essenes were thus led to the wilderness by the same scriptural directions that motivated the life and ministry of John. The early Christians understood John as " 'the voice of one crying in the wilderness: Prepare the way of the Lord, make his paths straight'" (Mark 1:3). This passage from Mark quotes the same words from Isaiah 40:3 that are quoted in the Qumran Manual of Discipline.

The Qumran settlement and the adjacent caves where the

scrolls were found are located in the vicinity of the traditional place of John's activity near Jericho. Luke's account of
John's birth ends with the astonishing remark: "And the child
grew and became strong in spirit, and he was in the wilderness till the day of his manifestation to Israel" (Luke 1:80).
How could this little child, the only son of aged parents,
grow up in the wilderness? Well, the Essenes lived there,
leading a kind of monastic life. According to Josephus they
would receive the children of other people when they were
"still young and capable of instruction" and would care for
them as their own and raise them according to their way of
life. It would seem that John the Baptist was raised at Qumran—or at a place very much like it—until he became the
voice of one crying in the wilderness, calling for repentance.

Correspondences between the life and teachings of the
Qumran community and the life and teachings of John are
often extraordinary. John's baptism, as we learn from the
Gospels, is but the outward sign of the reality of repentance
and the assurance of God's forgiveness (Mark 1:4). After the
penitent people had confessed their sins, John baptized
them. This probably consisted of immersion in the waters of
the Jordan River. However, without the "fruit worthy of repentance" (Matthew 3:8), this rite of purification was useless; as Josephus puts it: "The soul must be already thor-
oughly cleansed by righteousness." In the Manual of
Discipline (3:3–8) we read that cleansing of the body must
be accompanied by purification of the soul. Someone who is
still guided by the stubbornness of his heart, who does not
want to be disciplined in the community of God, cannot become holy, but instead remains unclean, even if he should
wash himself in the sea or in rivers; for he must be cleansed
by the holy spirit and by the truth of God.

The Teacher of Righteousness

According to the Gospels, John the Baptist announced the
coming of a "Stronger One" who would baptize with the
Holy Spirit and with fire (Mark 1:7–8). The Qumran community had a similar expectation: They anticipated that their
ritual washings would be superseded with a purification by

the Holy Spirit at the end of time; then God himself will pour his spirit like water from heaven and remove the spirit of perversion from the hearts of his chosen people. Then they would receive the "knowledge of the Most High and all the glory of Adam" (Manual of Discipline 4:20–22).

In Matthew 21:32, we read that Jesus himself said that "John came to you in the way of righteousness, and you did not believe him . . . [E]ven when you saw it, you did not afterwards repent and believe him." Similarly with the high priests and elders in Jerusalem who did not accept John (Matthew 21:23–27). John may be compared with the most influential man in the Qumran movement, the Teacher of Righteousness. This great anonymous figure announced the events that would come upon the last generation, but the

Josephus on the Essenes

The first-century Jewish historian Josephus describes the monastic ways and ragged appearance of the Essenes, which are strikingly similar to the portrayal of John the Baptist in the New Testament.

Among the Jews there are three schools of thought, whose adherents are called Pharisees, Sadducees, and Essenes respectively. The Essenes profess a severer discipline: they are Jews by birth and are peculiarly attached to each other. They eschew pleasure-seeking as a vice and regard temperance and mastery of the passions as virtue. Scorning wedlock, they select other men's children while still pliable and teachable, and fashion them after their own pattern—not that they wish to do away with marriage as a means of continuing the race, but they are afraid of the promiscuity of women and convinced that none of the sex remains faithful to one man. Contemptuous of wealth, they are communists to perfection, and none of them will be found to be better off than the rest: their rule is that novices admitted to the sect must surrender their property to the order, so that among them all neither humiliating poverty nor excessive wealth is ever seen, but each man's possessions go into the pool and as with brothers their entire property belongs to them

people who "do violence to the covenant" did "not believe" his words (Commentary on Habakkuk 2:2–9).

The Teacher of Righteousness was the priest ordained by God to lead the repentant to the way of His heart. . . . His teaching was like that of a prophet, inspired by the holy spirit. John too was a priest, the son of the priest Zacharias (Luke 1:5). Like the Qumran Teacher of Righteousness, John separated himself from the priesthood in Jerusalem and from the service in the Temple. And, like the Teacher of Righteousness, he was also a prophet.

Both the Teacher of Righteousness and John the Baptist nevertheless remained faithful to the laws of purity; they both practiced them in a radical, even ascetic, way. Both the Teacher of Righteousness and John the Baptist believed that

all. Oil they regard as polluting, and if a man is unintentionally smeared with it he scrubs himself clean; for they think it desirable to keep the skin dry and always to wear white. Men to supervise the community's affairs are elected by show of hands, chosen for their tasks by universal suffrage.

They possess no one city but everywhere have large colonies. When adherents arrive from elsewhere, all local resources are put at their disposal as if they were their own, and men they have never seen before entertain them like old friends. And so when they travel they carry no baggage at all, but only weapons to keep off bandits. In every town one of the order is appointed specially to look after strangers and issue clothing and provisions. In dress and personal appearance they are like children in the care of a stern tutor. Neither garments nor shoes are changed till they are dropping to pieces or worn out with age. Among themselves nothing is bought or sold: everyone gives what he has to anybody in need and receives from him in return something he himself can use; and even without giving anything in return they are free to share the possessions of anyone they choose.

Josephus, *The Jewish War* 2.125. Trans. G.A. Williamson. New York: Penguin Books, 1981, pp. 133–34.

the messianic age and the final judgment were soon to come. That is why they both practiced the purification of body and soul in such a strict way. The prophetic call for repentance and the apocalyptic expectation of the end of history led to the radicalization and generalization of the priestly laws of purity.

We are told that John the Baptist "did not eat nor drink" (Matthew 11:18), which means that he lived an ascetic life, eating locusts and wild honey (Mark 1:6), foods found in the desert. John wanted to be independent, unpolluted by civilization, which he considered unclean. In this he was not unlike the Essenes living at Qumran. John's cloak was made of camel's hair and the girdle around his waist was leather, well suited to his aim of strict purity. . . .

John's preaching had several characteristics that can also be found at Qumran. For example, John used prophetic forms of rebuke and threat (Matthew 3:7–10). The hypocrites who came to him for baptism without repenting he called "a brood of vipers" (Matthew 3:7). I believe this strange term is the Hebrew equivalent of *ma'ase 'eph'eh* or "creatures of the Snake"—that is, Sons of the Devil. This same phrase occurs in the Thanksgiving Hymns from Qumran (1QH 3:17). In short, the prophetic language of John the Baptist was enriched by the polemics of the Qumran community of Essenes.

The Opposing View

While there are thus many reasons to suppose that John the Baptist was an Essene who may have lived at Qumran, there are also impediments to this conclusion that must be as assiduously pursued as the correspondences. First, John is never mentioned in the Dead Sea Scrolls that have been published so far.

Perhaps more telling is the fact that John is never called an Essene in either the New Testament or in Josephus. The absence of such a reference is especially significant in Josephus, because in both *Antiquities of the Jews* and *The Jewish War*, Josephus discusses the Essene sect several times as a Jewish "philosophy," on a par with the Sadduccees and the Pharisees. In *The Jewish War* (2:567), Josephus even mentions another John, whom he identifies as "John, the Essene," who served as a Jewish general in the First Jewish Revolt against Rome. Josephus also identifies three prophetic figures as Essenes (although he does not call them prophets). All of this indicates that Josephus would have identified John the Baptist as an Essene if he knew him to be a member of that group.

Even more significantly, John the Baptist was outspokenly critical of the civil government, which would be uncharacteristic of an Essene. The Baptist went so far as to criticize the tetrarch Antipas himself for marrying his "brother's wife" (Mark 6:18). With his preaching, John created such excitement among the crowds that Herod became afraid that this might lead to a revolt. John's outspokenness seems unlike an Essene. . . .

But this is not the end of the discussion. There is a way to reconcile both the pros and cons. As Josephus reminds us, not all Essenes led a monastic life in the wilderness of Judah. Indeed some sound almost like John the Baptist. Josephus even speaks of Essene prophets. Nor were these pseudo-prophets, impostors and deceivers, of whom Josephus has much to say, but men who foresaw and told the truth, much like the classic prophets of ancient Israel. These Essene seers appeared suddenly, standing up to kings, criticizing their conduct or foretelling their downfall. Josephus does not describe their teaching and way of life; he simply characterizes them as Essenes.

In short, there is no clear-cut conflict between the priestly way of life (Essene) and the prophetic. Both biblical traditions—the priestly and the prophetic one—influenced the Essenes just as they did John the Baptist.

I believe that John grew up as an Essene, probably in the desert settlement at Qumran. Then he heard a special call of God; he became independent of the community—perhaps even more than the Essene prophets described by Josephus. With his baptism of repentance, John addressed all Israel directly; he wanted to serve his people and to save as many of them as possible.

The Essenes of Qumran no doubt prepared the way for

this prophetic voice in the wilderness. They succeeded in combining Israel's priestly and prophetic heritage in a kind of eschatological existence. The Essenes radicalized and democratized the concept of priestly purity; they wanted a true theocracy and they sought to turn the people of God into a "kingdom of priests" (Exodus 19:5–6). . . .

This was true as well for John the Baptist. He was the son of a priest and practiced the laws of priestly purity in a radical way. But in his ministry for Israel he acted as a prophet . . . to announce the coming of the Messiah. In his baptism, both traditions were combined, just as they were in the Essene philosophy: The priestly laws of ritual purity were combined with the prophetic concern for repenting, returning to God, and offering oneself to Him. Accordingly, it is reasonable to conclude that John the Baptist was raised in the tradition of the Essenes and may well have lived at Qumran before taking his message to a wider public.

The Life of Jesus

E.P. Sanders

> E.P. Sanders, arts and sciences professor of religion at
> Duke University, is the author of the critically acclaimed
> books *Paul and Palestinian Judaism* (1977) and *Jesus and Ju-
> daism* (1985). In this brief but comprehensive sketch from
> his 1993 book, *The Historical Figure of Jesus*, he summa-
> rizes the life of the central figure of the Christian religion.
> Topics covered include the time and place of Jesus' birth,
> where he preached, and his relationship with John the
> Baptist. Sanders also discusses Jesus' move to Jerusalem,
> where he angered the authorities, his arrest, execution,
> and the account by his disciples of his resurrection, which
> provided the basis for belief by later converts that he was
> a divine being.

There are no substantial doubts about the general course of
Jesus' life: when and where he lived, approximately when
and where he died, and the sort of thing that he did during
his public activity. When we begin to probe beneath the surface, difficulties and uncertainties arise, but for the present
we shall stay on the surface. I shall first offer a list of statements about Jesus that meet two standards: they are almost
beyond dispute; and they belong to the framework of his life,
and especially of his public career. (A list of everything that
we know about Jesus would be appreciably longer.)

> Jesus was born *c.* 4 BCE, near the time of the death of
>   Herod the Great;
> he spent his childhood and early adult years in Nazareth, a

Galilean village [Note: Galilee was a Palestinian region located north of Judaea];

he was baptized by John the Baptist;

he called disciples;

he taught in the towns, villages and countryside of Galilee (apparently not the cities);

he preached 'the kingdom of God';

about the year 30 he went to Jerusalem for Passover;

he created a disturbance in the Temple area;

he had a final meal with the disciples;

he was arrested and interrogated by Jewish authorities, specifically the high priest;

he was executed on the orders of the Roman prefect, Pontius Pilate.

We may add here a short list of equally secure facts about the aftermath of Jesus' life:

his disciples at first fled;

they saw him (in what sense is not certain) after his death;

as a consequence, they believed that he would return to found the kingdom;

they formed a community to await his return and sought to win others to faith in him as God's Messiah. . . .

When Was Jesus Born?

Now I shall supplement the outline with a short narrative summary.

The year of Jesus' birth is not entirely certain. . . . Most scholars, I among them, think that the decisive fact is that Matthew dates Jesus' birth at about the time Herod the Great died. This was in the year 4 BCE, and so Jesus was born in that year or shortly before it; some scholars prefer 5, 6 or even 7 BCE.

That Jesus was born a few years before the beginning of the era that starts with his birth is one of the minor curiosities of history. In this work I use the letters BCE and CE to mean 'Before the Common Era' and 'Common Era'. ('Common' means 'accepted by all, including non-Christians'.) The traditional abbreviations, however, are BC and

AD, 'Before Christ' and 'Anno Domini' ('in the year of the Lord'). These letters divide history into years before Jesus was born and after his birth. How, then, could he have been born 4 BC (or BCE)? In the sixth century a Scythian monk who was resident in Rome, Dionysius Exiguus, introduced a liturgical calendar that counted years 'from the incarnation' (the birth of Jesus) rather than according to the system established by the pagan Roman emperor Diocletian. Dionysius' information, however, was limited. He could fix neither the death of Herod (Matt. 2) nor the census of Quirinius (Luke 2) precisely, and he seems to have made an estimate based on other information in Luke: John the Baptist, who preceded Jesus, began preaching in the fifteenth year of Tiberius (Luke 3.1); Jesus was about thirty years old when he began his ministry (Luke 3.23). The fifteenth year of Tiberius was (by modern reckoning) 29 CE; if Dionysius Exiguus allowed one year for John the Baptist's mission, he would have concluded that Jesus began his ministry in 30 CE. If Jesus was precisely thirty years old at the time, he was born in the year 1. This is probably the reasoning that led to our present calendar. Modern scholars note that Jesus' age in Luke 3.23 is a round number, and that Luke as well as Matthew sets the beginning of the story 'in the days of Herod the king' (Luke 1.5). As I just indicated, this seems to be the firmest piece of evidence regarding the time of Jesus' birth. The calendar based on Dionysius' calculation, however, which was not based on the date of Herod's death, gained general support in the sixth and subsequent centuries, with the result that scholars now date Jesus' birth a few years 'Before Christ'.

Jesus and John

Jesus lived with his parents in Nazareth, a Galilean village. One of Herod the Great's heirs, Antipas, was the ruler of Galilee for the entirety of Jesus' life (except for the very earliest period, when Herod the Great was still alive). It is a strong possibility that virtually all of Jesus' active ministry, except the last two or three weeks, was carried out in Antipas' Galilee. Jesus was not an urbanite. The cities of Galilee—

Sepphoris, Tiberias and Scythopolis (Hebrew, Beth-Shean)—do not figure in the accounts of his activities. He doubtless knew Sepphoris, which was only a few miles from Nazareth, but he nevertheless seems to have regarded his mission as being best directed to the Jews in the villages and small towns of Galilee. Nazareth itself was quite a small village. It was in the hill country, away from the Sea of Galilee, but Jesus taught principally in the villages and towns on the sea. Some of his followers were fishermen. Rural images are fairly frequent in the teaching that is ascribed to him.

When Jesus was a young man, probably in his late twen-

Jesus' Arrest and Trial

In this excerpt from her informative and handsomely illustrated book, The World of the Bible, *biblical scholar Roberta Harris discusses the archaeological evidence gathered to date about the locations of Jesus' arrest and trial.*

Both the Sadducees and the Pharisees wanted Jesus arrested and executed for sedition, but were cautious about acting publicly. After celebrating the Last Supper, Jesus and the apostles left Jerusalem to return to Bethany, stopping to pray in a peaceful garden on the Mt of Olives, just outside the city beyond the Kidron valley. This was the garden of Gethsemane (Gath Shemen), where Jesus was arrested by the Romans with the help of Judas Iscariot.

Today there is still a quiet olive grove in the grounds of the Church of All Nations. The olive trees, though ancient, are not 2,000 years old. Titus, the Roman general and later emperor, who destroyed Jerusalem in AD 70, had most trees in and around the city cut down. New trees probably sprang from the old, however, and the present gardens lie beside the ancient path to the mountain summit and the route to Bethany. Jesus must have been arrested nearby.

Jesus was first questioned in the House of Caiaphas, the High Priest, somewhere in the Upper City. The next morning he was handed over to the Romans for trial and sentence. For

ties, John the Baptist began preaching in or near Galilee. He proclaimed the urgent need to repent in view of the coming judgement. Jesus heard John and felt called to accept his baptism. All four gospels point to this as an event that transformed Jesus' life. According to Mark's account, Jesus 'saw the heavens opened and the Spirit descending upon him like a dove'; he also heard a voice saying, 'You are my beloved son' (Mark 1.9–11).

Antipas arrested John because he had criticized his marriage to Herodias (the gospels) or because he feared that the Baptist's preaching would lead to insurrection (Josephus)—or

---

centuries it was thought that the imprisonment and trial of Jesus took place in the Antonia fortress at the northwestern corner of the Temple Mount. This was one of the chief Roman positions in the city and an underground tunnel led from it directly into the Temple area. A Roman pavement in the cellar of the Convent of the Sisters of Zion was identified as the pavement (*lithostraton* in Greek or Gabbatha in Aramaic) where Pilate judged Jesus. Spanning the street outside the Convent is an arch known as 'Ecce Homo' ('Behold the man'). Here, it was believed, was the spot where Pilate showed Jesus to the crowd.

The street running below the arch towards the Church of the Holy Sepulchre is traditionally called the Via Dolorosa ('Way of Grief') and the 12 Stations of the Cross are marked for pilgrims. Today, with a better understanding of the topography and chronology of Jerusalem in the 1st century AD, we know that these traditional identifications are mistaken.

Most scholars now believe that Jesus' trial was held in Herod's palace, on the northwestern edge of the city, which by that time was the headquarters of the Roman prefect when he was in Jerusalem. He always came up from his seat in Caesarea to be present in Jerusalem for the festivals, bringing with him a large troop of soldiers in case of trouble.

Roberta L. Harris, *The World of the Bible*. New York: Thames and Hudson, 1995, pp.147–48.

both. At about that time Jesus began his public ministry. Whereas John had worked outside settled areas, Jesus went from town to town, village to village, usually preaching in synagogues on the sabbath. He called a small number of people to be his disciples, and they joined him in his travels. Unlike John, Jesus not only preached but also healed the sick. He developed a reputation, and people thronged to see him. Soon he too had to preach in open areas because of the crowds.

Death and Resurrection

We do not know just how long this itinerant ministry continued, but apparently it lasted only one or possibly two years. After preaching and healing for this period of time in Galilee, Jesus, with his disciples and some other followers, went to Jerusalem for Passover. Jerusalem was in Judaea, which, unlike Galilee, was a Roman province. Jerusalem itself was governed by the Jewish high priest, who was responsible to a Roman prefect. Jesus rode into the city on an ass, and some people hailed him as 'son of David'. When he went to the Temple, he attacked the money-changers and dove-sellers. The high priest and his advisers determined that Jesus was dangerous and had to die. After the Passover meal with his disciples, Jesus went apart to pray. One of his followers had betrayed him, and the high priest's guards arrested him. He was tried, after a fashion, and turned over to the Roman prefect, with the recommendation that he be executed. After a brief hearing, the prefect ordered his execution. He was crucified as an insurgent, along with two others.

He died after a relatively brief period of suffering. A few of his followers placed him in a tomb. According to some reports, when they returned two days later to anoint his body, they found the tomb empty. Thereafter his followers saw him. These resurrection experiences convinced them that Jesus would return and that in Jesus' life and death God had acted to save humanity. The disciples began to persuade others to put their faith in Jesus. They gave him various titles, including 'Anointed' (which is 'Messiah' in Hebrew and 'Christ' in Greek), 'Lord' and 'Son of God'. These titles reveal that, as the decades passed, Jesus' disciples and their converts developed various views of Jesus' relation to God and of his significance in God's plan for Israel and the world. Their movement finally separated from Judaism and became the Christian church. When the gospels were written, however, Christology (theological explanations of the person and work of Jesus) was at an early stage, and the separation of Christianity from Judaism not yet complete.

Chapter 2

The Growth and Spread of Christianity

Turning|Points

IN WORLD HISTORY

How Jesus' Apostles Helped Spread Christianity

Justo L. Gonzalez

The term "apostles" is sometimes limited to the twelve disciples who accompanied Jesus in his travels. More often, however, the term is used to describe those of Jesus' followers who, in the years immediately following his death, embarked on missions to spread the word that he was the Son of God. Some of these missionaries were members of the original twelve disciples and some were not. Except for the case of Paul, about whom a fair amount is known, little for certain is known about the travels and exploits of the other major early apostles. In this essay, noted religious scholar Justo Gonzalez, author of a well-reviewed three-volume work on the development of Christian thought, presents the chief facts and legends surrounding these important but sparsely documented early Christian figures.

The New Testament gives no indication as to the career of most of the apostles. Acts tells of the death of James, the brother of John. But that very book, after following Paul's career for a number of years, abruptly leaves him while preaching in Rome, awaiting trial. What became of Paul, Peter, and the other apostles? From an early date, traditions began to appear claiming that one or another of them had preached in a particular region, or had suffered martyrdom in one way or another. Most of these traditions are no more than the result of the desire of a church in a particular city to claim an apostolic origin. Others are more worthy of credit.

Excerpted from *The Story of Christianity*, vol. 1, *The Early Church to the Dawn of the Reformation*, by Justo L. Gonzalez. Copyright ©1985 by Justo L. Gonzalez. Reprinted by permission of HarperCollins Publishers, Inc.

Peter, Paul, and John

Of all these traditions, the most trustworthy is the one that affirms that Peter was in Rome, and that he suffered martyrdom in that city during the Neronian persecution. On these points, several writers of the first and second centuries agree. We are also told that he was crucified—according to one version, upside-down—and this seems to agree with the otherwise obscure words in John 21:18–19.

The case of Paul is somewhat more complex. The book of Acts leaves him while preaching in Rome. Ancient writers agree that he died in Rome—probably beheaded, as befitted a Roman citizen—at the time of Nero. But others say that he undertook some journeys that are not mentioned in Acts, including a trip to Spain. Some have tried to join these two traditions by supposing that Paul went to Spain between the end of Acts and the Neronian persecution. But this explanation encounters chronological difficulties. At best, all that can be said is that nothing is known for certain between the end of the book of Acts and Paul's death during the reign of Nero.

The task of reconstructing John's later career is complicated by the frequency with which the name of John appears in early records. There is an ancient tradition that claims that John was killed in a pot of boiling oil. But the book of Revelation places John, at about the same time, in exile on the island of Patmos. Another very trustworthy tradition speaks of John as a teacher at Ephesus, where he died around A.D. 100. All this indicates that there were at least two people with the same name, and that later tradition confused them. A second-century Christian writer—Papias of Hierapolis—affirms that there were indeed two persons by the name of John in the early church: one the apostle, and another an elder at Ephesus, who received the visions of Patmos. In any case, there was indeed towards the end of the first century, in the city of Ephesus, a Christian teacher named John, whose authority was great in all the churches of Asia Minor.

Late in the second century, a development took place that greatly hinders the task of the historian who seeks to discern the later career of the apostles. What happened was that the churches in every important city began claiming apostolic origins. In her rivalry with Rome and Antioch, the church in Alexandria felt constrained to have an apostolic founder, and thus the tradition appeared according to which Saint Mark had founded the church there. Likewise, when Constantinople became a capital city in the Empire, its church too needed apostolic roots, and thus it was claimed that Philip had preached in Byzantium, the ancient site where Constantinople was later built.

The Apostles in Spain?

There are other traditions regarding apostolic activities that are worthy of note, if not for their truthfulness, at least for their popularity and their significance for later history. This is particularly true of the traditions regarding the origins of Christianity in Spain and India.

Christians in Spain have claimed that their land was missionized, not only by Paul, but also by seven envoys of Saint Peter and by Saint James. The legend regarding Peter's missionaries to Spain appeared in the fifth century, but it was not as influential as that of James' visit to the country, which originated three centuries later. According to this tradition, James proclaimed the Gospel, without much success, in Galicia and Saragossa. On his way back, the Virgin appeared to him standing on a pillar, and gave him words of encouragement—this is the origin of the "Virgen del Pilar," still venerated by many in the Spanish tradition. Back in Jerusalem, James was beheaded by Herod, and then his disciples took his remains back to Compostela in Spain, where they are supposedly buried to this day.

This legend has been of great significance for the later history of Spain, for St. James (in Spanish, Santiago) became the patron saint of the nation. During the wars against the Moors, the name of "Santiago" was often the battle cry to which various small kingdoms rallied. At the same time, pilgrimages to the shrine of St. James in Compostela played an important role both in European religiosity and in the unification of northern Spain. The Order of Saint James was also a significant factor in Spanish history. Thus, although it is highly unlikely that James ever gave any thought to Spain, the legends regarding his visit were very influential in the later history of that country.

Thomas Visits India?

The tradition that claims Thomas visited India leaves historians somewhat baffled. It appears for the first time in the *Acts of Thomas*, which may have been written as early as the end of the second century. But already it is embellished with legendary tales, which make the entire account suspicious. We are told that an Indian king, Gondophares, was seeking an architect to build a palace, and that Thomas, who was no architect, offered himself for the job. When the king found that Thomas was giving to the poor the money allotted for the construction of the palace, he had the apostle put in prison. But then Gondophares' brother, Gad, died and came back from the dead. Upon his return he told his brother of the magnificent heavenly palace that he had seen, which was being built through Thomas' gifts to the poor. The king and his brother were then converted and baptized, and Thomas moved on to other parts of India, until he died as a martyr.

Obviously, much in this legend is of questionable authenticity, and historians have often discarded the whole of it as fictitious, for history had no record of Gondophares nor of any of the other details of the story. More recently, however, coins have been found that prove that there was indeed a ruler by that name, and that he had a brother named Gad. This, coupled with the undeniable antiquity of Christianity in India, and with the fact that at the time there was significant trade between India and the Near East, makes it more difficult to reject categorically the possibility that Thomas may have visited that land, and that later the story may have been embellished with all kinds of legendary accounts. In any case, it is significant that from a relatively early date there was a church in India, and that this church has repeatedly claimed Thomas as its founder.

In conclusion, it is certain that some of the apostles—particularly Peter, John, and Paul—did travel proclaiming the Gospel and supervising the churches that had been founded, either by them or by others. Perhaps other apostles, such as

Thomas, did likewise. But most of the traditions regarding apostolic travels date from a later period, when it was believed that the apostles divided the world among themselves, and when the church in each country or city sought to claim apostolic origins. In truth, most of the missionary work was not carried out by the apostles, but rather by the countless and nameless Christians who for different reasons—persecution, business, or missionary calling—traveled from place to place taking the news of the Gospel with them.

St. Paul's Mission to Spread the Christian Message

Michael Grant

More than any other single figure, Christianity owes its growth and success to the apostle Paul. Though he never met Jesus, Paul became a fanatical Christian devotee and missionary whose most brilliant and far-reaching act was to bring Jesus' teachings to the gentiles, who made up the majority of the population of the Mediterranean world at the time. In this masterful essay, the popular and prolific classical historian Michael Grant surveys Paul's life and contributions, including his religious ideas and writings. Grant also explains the rivalry between the Jewish and gentile Christian groups that ended with the Romans' destruction of Jerusalem and the subsequent survival and triumph of the gentile Christians.

Three days after Jesus's death on the cross, his followers believed that they saw him resurrected upon the earth and that he then ascended to heaven. And thus had begun the process by which the failure of his lifetime was converted into triumph after his death—one of the few revolutions in the world's history that has lasted.

But Jesus's posthumous triumph took a long time to become manifest. That it took place at all was due to the extraordinary accident, or act of providence, that made a man of towering gifts into one of the disciples of the crucified Jesus. He was Paul, a Jew of quite different origins from his new master, for whereas Jesus came from Galilee, an ap-

Reprinted with the permission of Scribner, a division of Simon & Schuster, from *History of Rome*, by Michael Grant. Copyright ©1978 by Michael Grant.

pendage of the homeland, Paul belonged to the Dispersion (Diaspora), comprising the communities of Jews in countries other than Palestine. The first Dispersion had taken place in the early sixth century B.C. after Jerusalem and its Temple had been destroyed by the Babylonians, who took many thousands of Jews away into foreign captivity. Some, later, were repatriated by the Persians who succeeded to the Babylonian Empire, but the Dispersion continued to increase in numbers, particularly when the Ptolemies introduced many Jews into their new city of Alexandria and then again when the Seleucids, who took their place as rulers of Palestine, settled many families in Asia Minor and subsequently drove many more out of Judaea by persecution. By the time of Paul, the Jews of the Dispersion were to be numbered in millions, comprising a sizable minority in many or most of the principal cities of the eastern Roman provinces.

Paul's Background

Paul himself came from the self-governing Greek city of Tarsus in Cilicia (southeastern Asia Minor). He claimed descent from the Jewish tribe of Benjamin and belonged to a family of strict Pharisees. It seems probable that he spent his youth at his native town, learning his father's craft of weaving goat's hair into tents, carpets, and shoes. Tarsus was a center of advanced Hellenic [Greek] culture, so that Paul was familiar with Greek and wrote in that language. The Jews in Greek cities like Tarsus were accorded a quasi-autonomous community status by the Roman authorities. But Paul's family enjoyed a more unusual distinction as well. They were among that section of the local population, never numerous in such towns, that had been granted Roman citizenship. Perhaps it was Paul's father who had acquired this franchise, either as a reward for services to Rome or because he had been a slave and was subsequently freed. At all events, although he gave his son the Jewish name of Saul, this was replaced, on occasion, by a Latin equivalent, Paulus—probably chosen because of its resemblance to his original name. Thus the young man possessed the remarkable triple qualification of belonging to the Jewish, Greek, and Roman civilizations all at the same time; no one else in ancient history spans, as he does, all those three different worlds.

But above all, he was a Jew, and a very active one; indeed he may well have been a member of an ultrapious group active in the Dispersion. At all events, soon after the crucifixion, he began to object strongly to Jesus's disciples and the Messianic claims they were putting forward on his behalf. In accordance with the coercive powers that the Romans delegated to their Councils at Jerusalem and elsewhere, the Jewish authorities were pursuing fierce sanctions against these dissidents. And in enforcing these sanctions, Paul tells us that he, himself, played an active part; perhaps he received his instructions from the local Council at Tarsus or Antioch and set out from one of these cities on his punitive missions.

Conversion and Early Preaching

In any case it was on one such disciplinary journey, perhaps in about A.D. 36, that he made for Damascus, an important "free" city of Syria that contained a Jewish community of considerable size. It was the devotees of Jesus among their number whom Paul had been commissioned by his Jewish chiefs to bring to order. But instead—he later declared— while he was on his way to Damascus, a mighty light flashed upon him and blinded him and felled him to the ground; and at the same time he heard a voice. Psychologists describe such experiences under the name of photism, a sensation of light or color accompanying some other species of sensation and especially a sound. The sound Paul believed that he heard was the voice of Jesus ordering him to enter Damascus where he would learn of a new task to perform. When he recovered, therefore, from his blindness, he went on into the city, where Jewish converts to Jesus's doctrines told him to go and preach to the Jews the glorious message (Gospel) that Jesus himself had been preaching to them a short while ago. And he gladly accepted this message since his experience outside the gates of Damascus had utterly changed his attitude to the followers of Jesus, so that, instead of being their remorseless persecutor, he now believed, no less fanatically, that they were right after all.

For what followed we have a remarkable source, the letters of Paul himself, written in Greek. The earliest of these documents perhaps dates back to about A.D. 50, only twenty years at most after the crucifixion of Jesus; so it antedates the first of the Gospels by at least sixteen and probably twenty years and constitutes by far the earliest Christian literature. Paul's vigorous, violent personality emerges from these epistles with stunning force; he was a strange addition indeed to the humble and uneducated adherents of the infant church. Despite his powerful intellect, he often wrote paradoxically and ambiguously—his letters were dashed off to meet the current needs of the moment, so that even the one with the greatest claims to a measure of comprehensiveness, the *Epistle to the Romans*, was not by any means intended as a systematic corpus of his views.

Furthermore, the letters were not primarily written with historical aims in mind. And yet they convey a great deal of invaluable information. Facts can also be derived from the *Acts of the Apostles*. . . .

The letters and the *Acts*, therefore, taken together, make it possible to give a fairly accurate idea of Paul's career and teaching. It becomes clear that, during the period immediately subsequent to his conversion, the embryonic Jewish movement that had accepted the Messiahship of Jesus was still based upon Jerusalem, the center of the Jewish faith and the place where Jesus had died. At first it was Peter, Jesus's close personal associate, who headed this Jewish Christian community and the fairly extensive missionary movement that it began to direct towards its fellow Jews in Judaea and neighboring lands. But in due course James the Just, the brother of Jesus, took Peter's place. After Paul had been converted, there was, for a time, no split between himself and this group, and he worked as its missionary to its fellow Jews, first in Arabia (southern Jordan) and later for ten years in Syria and Cilicia.

Mission to the Gentiles and Death

Then in about 45, with his friend Barnabas, he set out on the first of those far more widespread journeys of his, which so notably exploited the improved communications of the Pax Romana for the benefit of Christianity. This first great journey, lasting several years, took him not only to Syria but also to Cyprus and Asia Minor as well. The intention of Paul and Barnabas was to speak in synagogues to their fellow Jews. Yet matters did not turn out that way. For one thing the Jews were against Paul, since they objected to what they regarded as his deification of Jesus and the rejection of monotheism that this seemed to imply; and they carried their hatred of his teaching even to the lengths of physical violence. Furthermore, a strong disagreement arose between Paul and his own Jewish Christian mother church—a disagreement that before long caused the division of the Christian community into two virtually separate parts—one Jewish, and the other consisting of Gentiles, to whom Paul, rejected by the Jews, increasingly addressed his teaching. In particular, the Gentiles who accepted the new faith proved unwilling to un-

Paul's Conservative Social Views

Like other Jewish and Christian holy men of his day, Paul held conservative social views, reflecting the belief that church teachings about spirituality, chastity, and respect for authority provided a useful guide for people's everyday lives. Following is one such teaching, on slavery, widely viewed today as inhumane and exploitive.

Slaves, obey in everything those who are your earthly masters, not with eyeservice, as men-pleasers, but in singleness of heart, fearing the Lord.

Whatever your task, work heartily, as serving the Lord and not men, knowing that from the Lord you will receive the inheritance as your reward; you are serving the Lord Christ. For the wrongdoer will be paid back for the wrong he has done, and there is no partiality.

Masters, treat your slaves justly and fairly, knowing that you also have a Master in heaven.

Colossians 3.22–4.1; Timothy 2.8–15, Holy Bible, Revised Standard Version. New York: Thomas Nelson and Sons, 1952.

dergo circumcision and the dietary restrictions required of Jews; and whereas Paul saw no possibility of enforcing such practices upon them, the Jewish Christians deplored this permissive attitude. Nevertheless, he set out with a series of different companions on two further huge journeys during which he addressed himself once again ever increasingly to the Gentiles, who did not make such injurious objections. These travels covered a period of about eight years, including one and a half years spent at Corinth, in Greece, and three at Ephesus (Selçuk) on the west coast of Asia Minor.

On returning to Jerusalem in about A.D.58, Paul was subjected to accusations of blasphemy by the angry Jews, and the Roman authorities arrested him to save his life. While still detaining him at their provincial capital Caesarea Maritima (Sdot Yam), two successive Roman governors deferred a decision on these charges, anxious to evade the obscure but inflammable questions at issue. However, when Paul, as a Roman citizen, requested that his case should be transferred to the court of the emperor Nero at Rome, his appeal was granted; and after an eventful journey, including shipwreck at Melita (Malta), he spent two years in the city, first under informal house arrest and then in prison. Finally, following a trial or trials, instigated this time not by the Jews but apparently by his other enemies the Jewish Christians, he was condemned to death and executed, either in 64 when the Christian community at Rome was persecuted as scapegoats for the city's Great Fire, which had destroyed the city, or possibly a year or two later.

The Saving Power of the Resurrection

There was something wrong with Paul, what he called his "thorn in the flesh"—either a physical ailment or more probably a sexual problem, since although, like Jesus, he adopted the un-Jewish practice of enlisting women to help him in his ministry, he wrote somewhat sourly about sex. But the characteristic of Paul that most greatly struck the imagination of those who came after him was his fabulous perseverance and endurance. Wherever he went, he urgently argued, remonstrated, appealed in support of the new sort of

Judaism that he believed to have been made necessary and inevitable by Jesus's crucifixion. Oscillating strangely between modesty and self-confidence, he was unimpressive in presence and manner; but he hectoringly [heroically] repeated over and over again his demands for utter obedience.

It was obedience to a novel cause. The reason why Paul became converted was that he found he could no longer accept the normal Jewish view that the Torah was the answer to all the problems of life. Criticizing this whole code far more sharply than Jesus—who had merely stated that he came not to destroy the Law but to complete it—Paul denounced its provisions as over burdened with legalism and unrealistic in its demands for perfection. Like other Jews, Paul held that the Fall of Adam had plunged the whole world into evil ways. But unlike them, as he looked around at its ills and above all at the miseries of the Jewish people in their homeland, he felt that the Torah had, for centuries, failed to end these tribulations and was still failing to end them now; so it could not possibly be the answer he was looking for.

That being so, mere oral explications to its doctrines, such as the Pharisees were prepared to offer, did not seem enough; instead, a total change was needed, something that would turn the whole of this abominable history into complete and abrupt reverse. And in his desperate perplexity, although he had never known Jesus himself, Paul seized on the astonishing, moving tales of his Crucifixion and Resurrection and Ascension and decided that these reported events possessed exactly the saving power of reversal that he was looking for. That was not, obviously, the same as Jesus had preached, since when Jesus was preaching these events had not yet happened. Moreover, in strange contrast to the later Gospels, Paul is almost totally uninterested in any and every supposed occurrence in Jesus's life before the Last Supper. It was his death only, and what followed after his death, that Paul declared to be redemptive (by God's Grace, besides which he held all human initiatives to be negligible). He was very well aware that Jews and Greeks alike would find it singularly hard to understand that these happenings *have anything to do with us*. Yet that is what he believed, and what he devoted his life and eloquence to explaining to the outside world. In comparison with the central, overwhelming significance of the redemptive power of Jesus's death and what followed it, the whole Jewish code, in fact all knowledge in any ordinary sense of the word, seemed to him useless and pointless.

The Survival of the Gentile Christians

Yet many Jews and Jewish Christians alike considered that this rejection of the Law was nothing better than an open invitation to license, and they therefore refused to join him in throwing the Torah overboard. In consequence, both communities turned against him; and his career seemed to have ended in total failure. His churches for Gentile converts did not prosper, or even in many cases continue to exist. Instead, such Christian communities as survived in the Dispersion preferred to follow the Jewish Christian church, based on the very code he had spurned. His reputation at the time of his death was at its lowest ebb.

But then the course of events was remarkably changed by the First Jewish Revolt (A.D. 66–73). The province of Judaea had never been a credit to Rome. Elsewhere in the empire, Roman government, if sometimes unimaginative, had generally been relatively successful, or at least peaceable. In Judaea, on the other hand, successive provincial governors, men lacking senatorial rank and supported only by a small garrison of non-Jewish auxiliaries, had been obliged to grapple with an almost continuous and ever-worsening series of internal crises, embittered by mutual incomprehension of each other's religious attitudes. As a result, an underground terrorist movement developed, or rather several distinct movements; and finally the imprudent actions of one of the governors triggered off open revolt. With all the resources of the Roman Empire against them, the rebels had no chance of success. Besides, they chose the worst possible moment for themselves, when Rome had just made a durable peace with its eastern enemy Parthia. For a time, it is true, the Jewish insurgents were given a lucky reprieve by the prolonged Roman civil wars after Nero's death. But the end was bound to come, and the obliteration of Jerusalem and its Temple by Vespasian's son Titus in 70 marked the end of the nation's life in Israel for more than two thousand years.

When the Jews, because of this rebellion, fell into total disgrace with the Roman occupying power, the Christians in their midst urgently needed to convince the Romans that they themselves lacked any taint of Judaism. But in this respect the split in their ranks proved damaging. The Jewish Christians, despite all their efforts to prevent this, became discredited in Roman eyes along with the Jews; and so they dwindled gradually into a scattering of insignificant sects, which failed to survive into the modern world. The Gentile Christians, on the other hand, escaped this Roman stigma and lived on to become the dominant force and theme of the Christianity of the future. Within the first two decades following the revolt, it was they who produced all four Gospels: books that preach a sharp dissociation from the Jews and present the Jewish Christians, too, as exemplified by Jesus's apostles, in a very unfavourable light.

And so, because of this strange reversal of circumstances, Paul's Gentile mission had prevailed after all. True, much of his own teaching still seemed too daring and provocative, and the *Acts of the Apostles* which deals with his career says remarkably little, indeed virtually nothing, about the content of his message. Yet because his ministry had been directed to the Gentiles he had to be rehabilitated. The *Acts*, therefore, chooses to praise him, not for his embarrassing views, but on the safer grounds that he was an indefatigable missionary; and "the greatest example of endurance" was what he remained. . . .

By extending Christianity to the Gentiles, it was he who had made it into a world religion. And since then he has been the greatest single source of all its successive spiritual revivals. Whenever the faith has been in danger of flagging, the memory of the man who first spread it far and wide has been revived time after time to give it new life.

The Organization of the Early Church

Chester G. Starr

Chester G. Starr, Bentley Professor of History Emeritus of the University of Michigan, has written many authoritative books about the history, culture, and religions of the ancient Roman world, including *Civilization and the Caesars*. In this essay, Starr describes the development of early church organization, which was dominated by the powers, responsibilities, and duties of the bishops. These leaders, each of whom oversaw an individual Christian community, were key figures in developing the moral tone and policy of the Christian brotherhood as a whole. That brotherhood in many ways perpetuated Jewish ethical and kindly social practices such as caring for the sick and unfortunate and opposing what the faithful viewed as the social evils of the day.

The century after the deaths of Peter and Paul is the darkest in Christian history. The churches were still small and suffered from the dislike of pagans and Jews alike; disagreements over doctrine grew more intense as the generation which had known the disciples (with whom Paul was reckoned) vanished. Yet the firm promise of salvation offered by the Christian creed and its strongly ethical teachings, reinforced by the close bond of believers in each local nucleus, gave it an ever firmer foothold in the cities of the Empire and even in the countryside in the east; and the prosperity of the Empire permitted its emissaries to travel back and forth with relative ease.

During this period many of the fundamental qualities that marked Christianity through the rest of the Empire, and even later, were established. Of these we may examine those connected with its organization. . . .

Church Leaders

The church in each city—and Christianity was organized on the basis of the cities—was independent. Initially, like the synagogue, it had a fairly democratic organization under a board of elders (*presbyters*) and deacons; often too the ecstatic side of early Christianity was resected in the presence of local "prophets," who were filled with the divine spirit and communicated with God. As time went on, the general tendency of city government toward oligarchy [rule by a few powerful individuals] and the needs of the church itself for self-defense against persecution and heresy led to a concentration of powers. In the reign of Trajan the letters of Ignatius of Antioch assert that *presbyters* must be tuned to their bishop (*episkopos* or overseer) as the strings to a harp, and that a church must be unified under its bishop to be with God. Not all churches thus had single leaders even in the later second century, but by the third century the bishop of each city, though still elected, was the spokesman for and director of his congregation. Church history came to be organized on the chain of bishops reaching back to the apostolic foundation. The doctrine of Apostolic Succession, that is, that the powers given to the disciples by Christ before His Ascension were handed down from bishop to bishop by the sacrament of ordination, was already explicit by the end of the first century in the letter of Clement of Rome.

The bishop's responsibilities were many. In the first place he oversaw the regular ceremonies of worship or sacraments, which became more fixed and extensive. Baptism by triple immersion in the name of the Father, the Son, and the Holy Ghost came after study in Christian doctrine; only those so baptized could partake in the most sacred rite. This was the eucharist, originally an evening ceremony after a community meal (*agape*) and then shifted to the morning as an independent ceremony; it was accompanied, after the fashion of the synagogues, by prayers, hymns, and the reading of the Bible. At regular intervals the faithful thus commemorated the Last Supper and united in the sacrifice of Christ. Penance, which was not considered by the Epistles to the Hebrews as possible after baptism, slowly became a regular rite as a disciplinary and corrective measure. The sacraments, which eventually numbered seven, thus emerged as formal bonds of Christian brethren and as continuing reinforcement and guarantee of their faith. Salvation was possible only within the framework of the Church.

Coordinating Christian Belief and Policy

Second, the bishop administered through the deacons the property of his church, which came to encompass a meeting place, a cemetery, and the bequests of the faithful. From the famous, but brief attempt at communal living which Acts records, the Christian Church had a strong sense of social responsibility to care for the sick, for widows and orphans, and for the unfortunate. This social sense stood in strong contrast to the ruthless, atomistic quality of much of pagan life as did the firm grounding in Christian doctrine of the principle that all the children of God were equally endowed with an individual soul.

Both social principles helped to draw searching individuals into the fold, but the Church was not an egalitarian system in practice. It opposed licentiousness, suicide, exposure of newborn infants, and other social evils; yet it made no effort to preach revolution or even to oppose slavery in principle. Nor were all its members underprivileged. The unfortunate Ananias (Acts 5:1–10) had had property, and thereafter persons of wealth and culture formed a not unimportant element in the Christian community. If tradition can be trusted, even [the first-century emperor] Domitian's cousin, Flavius Clemens, consul [a high government official] in 95, and his wife Domitilla were Christians; more to the point, the bishops and thinkers of the Church were largely forceful, passably educated men.

Third, the bishop kept in contact with his fellow bishops to coordinate Christian belief and policy. To a large extent this communication was by messengers and by letters, following the precedent of Paul. The writer Tertullian, in proving the unity of the Church, commented on its "peaceful intercommunion, the title of brotherhood, and the fellowship of hospitality." In the late second century Avircius Marcellus of Phrygia, probably a bishop, traveled as far west as Rome: "I saw too the plain of Syria and all its cities, Nisibis beyond the Euphrates; and everywhere I found brethren, with [the writings of] Paul in my hands and Faith everywhere led the way" and prepared for him the eucharist, symbol of Christian unity.

Eventually councils of bishops came to meet for better debate. We know of such a council at Rome under [the second-century emperor] Commodus to handle the thorny question of settling the date for the increasingly popular festival of Easter. This controversy, incidentally, produced the first known effort of a bishop of Rome (Victor) to excommunicate those who disagreed with him as representative of the church of Peter and Paul. From the third century such meetings became more frequent as the Church grew stronger and was vexed by problems of heresy.

The Bishop of Rome's
Increasingly Strong Position

Since church organization tended to follow imperial divisions, the bishop of the capital city in each province often had pre-eminence; and, indeed, his church might well have been the original center from which Christianity spread to the countryside. After Jerusalem fell, the bishop of Rome, the imperial capital and center of communications, was in a particularly strong position, which was reinforced by the foundation of the Roman church by Peter; for all could read the words of Christ to Peter, "Thou art Peter [*Caipha* in Aramaic]; and upon this rock [*caipha* in Aramaic; *petra* in Greek] I will build my church . . . And I will give unto thee the keys of the kingdom of Heaven." Yet, though the famous bishop Cyprian of Carthage could hail the Roman church in 252 as "the chair of Peter and the leader whence priestly unity has been derived," his letter was a firm lecture to his fellow bishop at Rome; and in the next sentences he proclaimed the right of his church to set its own course. The implications of the doctrine of Petrine supremacy were only to be worked out long afterward; the phrase Catholic Church (*katholike ekklesia*) used from Ignatius onward meant at this time only the union of all believers.

Early Christian Worship

J.W.C. Wand

J.W.C. Wand, former bishop of London and a prolific chronicler of Christian history and literature, offers considerable detail about the development of such institutions as church buildings, holy days, and ecclesiastical (church) courts. He also explains how sacramental and official practices such as confession, communion, baptism, confirmation, and excommunication were conducted in the church's early years.

Until the third century services and meetings were held in private houses, as they had been originally in the upper room at Jerusalem. The church in a particular house would include the members of the family, the slaves and dependents, together with other Christians situated conveniently near. There might be several such small communities in one city. The insistence on the authority of the Bishop, which forms so marked a feature of second-century writings, had as part of its purpose the bringing of these various bodies under one central control. In the reign of [the third-century emperor] Alexander Severus, about 222, we begin to hear of special buildings being used as churches. The *Apostolic Constitutions* recommend an oblong structure looking to the East. Later a sanctuary and a narthex [passage or hall] were marked off, and during the more peaceful parts of the third century some of these ecclesiastical buildings became of considerable importance. Within the church was the Holy Table, behind which facing the people and with his presbyters on either hand sat the Bishop. Men and women sat apart, and each class had its own place assigned to it, Tertul-

Excerpted from J.W.C. Wand, *A History of the Early Church to A.D. 500* (London: Methuen, 1937). Copyright 1937 by J.W.C. Wand. Used courtesy of Random House UK.

lian being particularly horrified if a virgin should stray among the widows. Places were found for visitors befitting their rank and condition.

Dealing with Wrong-Doers

Worship from the earliest times consisted of the singing of hymns, reading of scriptures, prayers and Eucharist. It is generally thought that the Agape or love-feast was an original accompaniment of the Eucharist. But it is more probable that the Eucharist was always a purely ritual meal, and that the holding of a semi-sacred full meal began in unorthodox circles, not being introduced into the main stream of Church life until towards the end of the second century. Then it seems to have been a kind of community meal to which all contributed, and to have become a gift of charity from the rich to the poor before it was finally abandoned.

The attitude of the Church to the sinner within her fold was dictated by the threefold need to uphold a good example to the flock and to bear a good witness to those who were without as well as to restore the wrong-doer. The most difficult cases were those of people who had given way in persecution. . . . The other great difficulty was the case of those guilty of fleshly sins. . . . The *Didascalia* [an early Christian list of moral instructions and regulations] endeavours to keep the mean between harshness and laxity; it warns the Bishop against being afraid to bring the sinner under discipline and at the same time tells him that his business is not to condemn but to save. 'Judge severely, O Bishop, like Almighty God, and receive those who repent with compassion like God.' The guilty are to be excommunicated, and to be received back only after due penance.

Excommunication involved literally staying outside the church during the service. 'When he is put out, be not angry with him and contend with him, but let him keep outside of the church, and then let them go in and make supplication for him. . . . Then thou, O Bishop, command him to come in and thyself ask him if he repents. If he be worthy to be received into the Church, appoint him days of fasting according to his fault, two or three or five or seven weeks, and thus allow him to go, saying to him all that is proper for admonition and doctrine.'

An important element in this penitential system was the *exomologesis* or public confession of sin before the assembled congregation. This was part of a period of penance voluntarily entered upon. Where a sinner did not know whether he ought to submit to such a period of probation or not, advice could be sought in a private confession. If a sinner did not voluntarily seek discipline but was charged by a fellow-Christian (no charge from a heathen being admitted), the case was tried by a sort of court presided over by the bishop but so representative of the whole Church that even the laity seem to have taken a share in pronouncing judgment. It will be remembered that not only S. Paul but also the organisers of pagan clubs and *collegia* [social clubs, most often burial societies] condemned the practice of resort to the civil courts: it was held that the members of any brotherhood ought to be able to settle their differences among themselves. Cases that might come before the Christian bodies for jurisdiction were those of fraud, false witness, fleshly sins, homicide, heresy, schism, idolatry and magic. The severity of the period of penance imposed varied with different churches. The most elaborate system comes from Asia Minor, where we hear of three successive stages through which the penitent must pass. The first was that of the Hearers, who were dismissed from the Eucharist after the sermon; the second was that of the Kneelers, who stayed only a little longer while the congregation prayed over them; the last was that of the Consistents, who remained throughout the service but were not allowed to join in the oblation or to make their communion.

Holy Days and Communion

Penitential days and seasons to be observed by the whole Church came in very early. . . . Wednesday and Friday [were] set apart as station days, that is, days on which a special stand was made against the enemies of the soul. The custom was no doubt borrowed from the Jews, who kept Tuesdays and Thursdays in memory of Moses' journey up and down the Mount. The Christian days were those of the betrayal and crucifixion. 'When the Bridegroom shall be taken away then shall ye fast in those days.' The fast ended at three o'clock in the afternoon. In addition, a fast was kept annually on the Friday and Saturday of Holy Week. In the *Didascalia* this fast lasts for the whole of the week. Those who were to be baptised at Easter began their period of fasting forty days before, and it was probably this that led to our present practice of Lenten observance.

The earliest feasts to be observed were those of Easter and Sunday. The Easter festival lasted until Pentecost, and Tertullian mentions the custom of not kneeling for worship during that time. The Sunday was an Easter day in every week and was carefully distinguished from the Jewish sabbath. Until the time of Constantine there was no obligation to refrain from labour on that day, although Tertullian men-

---

The Apostles' Creed

Integral to the training of initiates and conducting of religious services in the early church was the Apostles' Creed, thought to have been set down by some of the original apostles in Jerusalem in the years directly following Jesus' death. Later Christian creeds, such as the Nicene, adopted in 325, were based on this earliest version.

1. I believe in God almighty
2. And in Christ Jesus, his only son, our Lord
3. Who was born of the Holy Spirit and the Virgin Mary
4. Who was crucified under Pontius Pilate and was buried
5. And the third day rose from the dead
6. Who ascended into heaven
7. And sitteth on the right hand of the Father
8. Whence he cometh to judge the living and the dead
9. And in the Holy Ghost
10. The holy church
11. The remission of sins
12. The resurrection of the flesh
13. The life everlasting.

Henry Bettenson, ed., *Documents of the Christian Church*. London: Oxford University Press, 1967, pp. 23–24.

tions the beginning of a pious effort in that direction. The characteristic note of the day was worship, and the essential element in that worship was the Eucharist.

The Eucharist or Thanksgiving was something quite different from the grace which Aristides tells us was said at every meal. It was the repetition of the rite which it was believed Jesus had instituted at the last meal of which He partook with His disciples. . . . When the practice of morning celebration began is not clear. . . . By Tertullian's day there was a general rule of fasting communion. The *Apostolic Constitutions* reveal the fact that children were accustomed to be present and to communicate. Non-communicating attendance was imposed upon the Consistents or highest class of penitents. For others than penitents . . . it was a highly prized privilege to receive the Sacrament each Sunday. Those who were sick were communicated at home. . . . During the times of persecution this duty exposed the messengers to special danger. There is a moving story of the young Tarcisius, who allowed himself to be done to death rather than deliver up the sacred Host that he was carrying. It was probably on account of this danger that there arose the custom of allowing the laity to take to their homes a sufficient supply of the consecrated Bread to last for some time. . . . Probably this custom did not last long. At any rate it was ultimately superseded by the practice of reserving the Sacrament in church.

As for the Liturgy in church, the central act began after the exclusion of penitents. . . . Then came the 'common prayers' and the kiss of peace. At the offertory the faithful brought their gifts of bread, upon which, together with the mixed chalice of wine and water brought by the deacons, the Bishop and presbyters laid their hands. The Bishop recited the Thanksgiving, to the precise words of which he was not tied down, and the whole congregation took their share in the act of consecration by reciting the great Amen. . . .

Baptisms were normally held only at Easter; and this sacrament of initiation, occurring only once in the Christian's life, was held in even greater esteem than was the Eucharist. It was led up to by a long preparation, though of course there was an exception to this in the case of infants.

Evidence for infant baptism becomes strong before the end of the second century. . . . But there were some, like Tertullian, who objected to the practice. By the middle of the third century Cyprian and others will not have children kept without the rite so long as eight days after their birth. They might be baptised at any time by clergy or, in case of necessity, by lay folk, and only those born just before Easter were brought to the great service. For adults a long period of catechumenate [pre-baptismal training] was necessary.

Even before being admitted to the catechumenate the postulant went through a long examination at the hands of the catechists. If he were the slave of a Christian, his master's consent and testimonial must be obtained. If he had a pagan master, he must be careful to please him. If he were a married man, he must be faithful; if he were unmarried, he must be chaste. If he were of unsound mind, he could receive no instruction until the malady was over—a provision that will not seem harsh if we remember the close connexion thought to prevail between insanity and demoniacal possession. The examination ended with a determined effort to see that the candidate was not pursuing any unlawful trade or profession. Then, if accepted, he was admitted to the catechumenate with the imposition of the hand.

After this ceremony the catechumen was considered as a Christian and had his own place in church, where he was allowed to remain for the Eucharist up to the end of the sermon. At the Agape he was not allowed to sit down with the faithful but was given a special cup and bread that had been exorcised. Normally he was kept under instruction for two or three years. The teaching would be twofold, moral and doctrinal. Of the former a sufficient example is given in the document on the 'Two Ways.'. . . Of the latter no complete example exists earlier than the fourth century, but its character can be judged from the Rule of Faith and its summary in the Apostles' Creed, the original form of which was the pattern for all baptismal creeds in the West.

Before Easter came round the catechists selected those sufficiently advanced for baptism, and put them through a second examination in which sponsors were called upon to witness to their moral fitness. Then throughout the forty days of Lent they were given more advanced instruction; also they were daily exorcised and subjected to fasting and penitential exercises. On the Wednesday in Holy Week the final examination took place before the Bishop. On Thursday they bathed, fasted on Friday, and on Saturday they were solemnly exorcised by the Bishop, who laid his hand on them, breathed on their face, and signed them with the cross. Before the Sunday there was an all-night vigil, and at cock-crow they were all taken to the baptistery where they undressed while the Bishop blessed the water and the oils.

After this each candidate in turn pronounced a renunciation of the devil and all his works. Then he was again exorcised, in Rome with oil and in Africa with the laying on of the hand. Finally he was taken down into the font, where he made a short confession of faith. The Bishop put to him the three main articles of the creed in question form, after each of which he baptised him, either by plunging him beneath the water or by pouring water over his head or by placing him beneath a jet. Then the newly baptised ascended from the font, and was anointed with the oil of thanksgiving, which by Tertullian is interpreted as giving him a share in the sacerdotal character of the Messiah.

Confirmation followed immediately upon baptism and was indeed a part of it. When all had been baptised, they repaired with the Bishop to the church. There he laid his hand upon them, prayed, anointed them with consecrated oil, signed them with the cross, and kissed them. This represents the Roman use. Elsewhere in the West there seems to have been no unction [application of holy oil], while in the East it was the imposition of the hand that disappeared.

After the Confirmation the Liturgy was resumed, the new members now for the first time taking part in the central act. A special feature introduced for their benefit was the offering with the bread and wine of two cups, one of water and the other of milk mingled with honey. After the thanksgiving these were administered to the new communicants to signify respectively their inward washing and the Promised Land into which they had entered.

The Writing of the New Testament

Owen Chadwick

In terms of religious writings, the word *canon* means an authoritative list of books, usually those that set down the standard rules and doctrines of a faith. The books of the New Testament, therefore, make up the second part of the Christian canon, the first part comprising the books of the Hebrew Old Testament. As explained here by Owen Chadwick, former Regius Professor of Modern History at Cambridge University, the New Testament canon accepted today was developed over a span of several hundred years. During these years, Chadwick writes, numerous works of dubious authenticity or worth were considered and rejected.

The Greek word *kanon* meant a ruler for measuring, and so, as a metaphor, any sort of rule or norm. So 'the canonical books' were the books which established 'a rule of faith', as distinct from other books which might be good but did not have the same authority.

When Jesus died the Jews had not yet quite settled what books ought to be in the Old Testament. Since the Christians did not yet have a New Testament, they did not use the name 'Old Testament' for the Jewish books; it is first found about AD 175 in a book by Melito Bishop of Sardis in Asia Minor, who was a good literary defender of his faith. But from the first, Christians had the idea of an old covenant between God and his people, through Abraham and Moses, and a new covenant through his Son. The Greek word *diatheke* used in the gospels means both a covenant and a will or testament. Until they had the name 'Old Testament', Christians called the books simply 'the Scriptures' or 'the Scripture'. Soon they began to give them an adjective, and say 'the holy Scriptures'. Sometimes they called the Old Testament 'the Law', because the Jews considered that part of it as the most important. But whatever they called it they used it constantly; it affected their style of Greek and religious ideas.

At first they did not need a New Testament, because there

The Muratorian Canon

This is an excerpt from the so-called Muratorian Canon, dated to circa A.D. 200 and written in poorly phrased Latin by an unknown scribe. A list of holy Christian writings of that time, it does not include some books that were later accepted into the New Testament.

The third book of the Gospel is that according to Luke. Luke, the physician, when, after the Ascension of Christ, Paul had taken him to himself as one studious of right wrote in his own name what he had been told, although he had not himself seen the Lord in the flesh. He set down the events as far as he could ascertain them, and began his story with the birth of John.

The fourth gospel is that of John, one of the disciples. . . . When his fellow-disciples and bishops exhorted him he said, 'Fast with me for three days from to-day, and then let us relate to each other whatever may be revealed to each of us.' On the same night it was revealed to Andrew, one of the Apostles, that John should narrate all things in his own name as they remembered them. . . .

Moreover the Acts of all the Apostles are included in one book. Luke addressed them to the most excellent Theophilus, because the several events took place when he was present; and he makes this plain by the omission of the passion of Peter and of the journey of Paul when he left Rome for Spain.

For the Epistles of Paul . . . he wrote to not more than seven

were still people alive who could remember what had happened, and the account was passed on by word of mouth. In this way it was distilled into words that were easy to remember—a story, a telling sentence. As the witnesses died they realized that they must collect the words in writing. The first three gospels show obvious signs of being made of a string of separate stories and sayings which those with memories had told.

To these were added letters from church leaders. For example, St Paul wrote a letter to the congregation at Corinth.

churches, in this order: the first to the Corinthians, the second to the Ephesians, the third to the Philippians, the fourth to the Colossians, the fifth to the Galatians, the sixth to the Thessalonians, the seventh to the Romans. . . . He wrote besides these one to Philemon, one to Titus, and two to Timothy. These were written in personal affection; but they have been hallowed by being held in honour by the Catholic Church for the regulation of church discipline. There are extant also a letter to the Laodiceans and another to the Alexandrians, forged under Paul's name to further the heresy of Marcion. And there are many others which cannot be received into the Catholic Church. For it is not fitting for gall to be mixed with honey.

The Epistle of Jude indeed, and two bearing the name of John, are accepted in the Catholic Church; also Wisdom, written by the friends of Solomon in his honour. We receive also the Apocalypse of John and that of Peter, which some of us refuse to have read in the Church. But the *Shepherd* was written very recently in our time by Hermas, in the city of Rome, when his brother, Bishop Pius, was sitting in the Chair of the Church of Rome. Therefore it ought also to be read; but it cannot be publicly read in the Church to the people, either among the Prophets, since their number is complete [?], or among the Apostles, to the end of time.

Henry Bettenson, ed., *Documents of the Christian Church*. London: Oxford University Press, 1967, pp. 28–29.

Someone would read it to the church meeting there. Then a copy would be made and passed on to help the next community; so it passed into 'Scripture'.

But other people besides Paul wrote letters. And other people wrote 'gospels', lives of Jesus. The Gnostics, who wanted to show that Jesus was not a real human being, wrote gospels. Legend makers whose joy was to list unlikely miracles wrote gospels of their own. These had to be winnowed out with some care: if a 'Gospel of Peter' turned up at a church meeting, it took knowledge to see that this was not the truth that the apostles taught, and that whichever Peter wrote it, this was not St Peter the apostle.

The separation of the books which belonged in the New Testament from other books which posed as apostolic took a long time—some 350 years in the end, though most of it was settled within a century and a half. Even up to about AD 180 they still had no proper list of books which should be read in church. Because they were illegal, they could not hold a council to decide the matter. It was done by the leaders of the churches, who used their good sense. It was easy to see that our four gospels came fairly directly from apostles and were the ones which ought to have authority, though there were some differences of opinion about the gospel of St John. Several of the letters of St Paul were easy, but everything else was uncertain for a time. At least one forged letter 'by an apostle' slipped through the net and got into the New Testament as the Second Epistle of St Peter.

Agreement by AD 400

A manuscript of the eighth century, written in appalling Latin on the basis of a vanished Greek text, and with its beginning lost, contains an early list of books. The original was probably written in Rome about AD 200. We know the list as the 'Muratorian canon' because the historian Lodovico Muratori found the document at the Ambrosian library of Milan in the eighteenth century. It is the earliest list that shows the New Testament as a 'finished' collection, though not quite as it stands today. There are the four gospels, with twelve Epistles of Paul, the Epistle of Jude, and two (not three as now) of John; the list still lacks the two Epistles of Peter, the Epistle to the Hebrews and the Epistle of St James. The writer considers, with some doubts, that the 'Apocalypse of Peter' should be in, but not the Shepherd of Hermas, a pleasant Roman book about forgiveness; perhaps the Wisdom of Solomon, which forms part of the Greek Old Testament, should be in the New Testament; and he accepts the Apocalypse of St John, our book of Revelation. From now on there was a Bible consisting of two parts, an Old Testament and a New. The Eastern Church favoured including the Epistle to the Hebrews, the West would not have it. The West liked the Revelation, which the East would still not have. By 400 the East accepted the Revelation and the West accepted Hebrews; so the New Testament was agreed.

Chapter 3

The Problems of Christianity

Defenders of the Early Christian Church

Will Durant

One of the most serious problems faced by early Christianity was an unfairly blackened reputation. This resulted from widespread belief among Roman pagans that Christians were criminals, baby killers, and cannibals who hated the human race. To dispel such claims, a number of educated Christians, who became known as the apologists, wrote long tracts explaining and defending Christian beliefs and practices. This well-informed essay, which concentrates on two of the greatest apologists—Tertullian and Origen—is by Will Durant, one of the most popular historians of the twentieth century. Durant is most famous for his eleven-volume historical series, *The Story of Civilization* (1935–1975), the tenth volume of which (*Rousseau and Revolution*, 1967) won the Pulitzer Prize. According to Durant, the apologists, especially Origen, did more than defend Christianity; they also helped to transform it from a simple set of religious beliefs and practices into a full-blown philosophy that could and did successfully compete with those accepted by Greek and Roman intellectuals.

The Church now won to its support some of the finest minds in the Empire. Ignatius, Bishop of Antioch, began the powerful dynasty of the post-apostolic "Fathers," who gave a philosophy to Christianity, and overwhelmed its enemies with argument. Condemned to be thrown to the beasts for refusing to abjure his faith (108), Justin composed on his way to Rome several letters whose hot devotion reveals the spirit in which Christians could go to their death:

> I give injunctions to all men that I am dying willingly for God's sake, if you do not hinder it. I beseech you, be not an unseasonable kindness to me. Suffer me to be eaten by the beasts, through whom I can attain to God. . . . Rather entice the wild beasts that they may become my tomb, and leave no trace of my body, that when I fall asleep I be not burdensome to any. . . . I long for the beasts that are prepared for me. . . . Let there come upon me fire and cross [crucifixion], struggles with wild beasts, cutting and tearing asunder, rackings of bones, mangling of limbs, crushing of my whole body, and cruel tortures of the devil, if so I may attain to Jesus Christ!

Quadratus, Athenagoras, and many others wrote "Apologies" for Christianity, usually addressed to the emperor. Minucius Felix . . . allowed his [pagan speaker] Caecilius to defend paganism ably, but made his [Christian opponent] Octavius answer him so courteously that Caecilius was almost persuaded to be a Christian. Justin of Samaria, coming to Rome in the reign of Antoninus [138–161], opened there a school of Christian philosophy, and, in two eloquent "Apologies," sought to convince the Emperor . . . that Christians were loyal citizens, paid their taxes promptly, and might, under friendly treatment, become a valuable support to the state. For some years he taught unmolested; but the sharpness of his tongue made him enemies, and in 166 a rival philosopher prodded the authorities to arrest him and six of his followers, and put them all to death. Twenty years later Irenaeus, Bishop of Lyons, struck a powerful blow for the unity of the Church in his *Adversus Haereses*, a blast at all heretics. The only way of preventing Christianity from disintegrating into a thousand sects, said Irenaeus, was for all Christians to accept humbly one doctrinal authority—the decrees of the episcopal councils of the Church.

Tertullian: From Defense to Attack

The doughtiest fighter for Christianity in this period was Quintus Septimius Tertullianus [popularly known as Tertul-

lian] of Carthage. Born there about 160, the son of a Roman
centurion, he studied rhetoric in the same school that
trained [the Roman novelist] Apuleius; then for years he
practiced law at Rome. Midway in life he was converted to
Christianity, married a Christian, renounced all pagan pleasures, and (says Jerome) was ordained a priest. All the arts
and tricks that he had learned from rhetoric and law were
now put at the service of Christian apologetics, enhanced by
a convert's ardor. Greek Christianity was theological, metaphysical, mystical; Tertullian made Latin Christianity ethical, juristic, practical. . . . Irenaeus had written in Greek;
with Minucius and Tertullian Christian literature in the
West became Latin, and Latin literature became Christian.

The Day of Judgment

In the year 197, while Roman magistrates in Carthage were
trying Christians on charges of disloyalty, Tertullian addressed to an imaginary court the most eloquent of his
works—the *Apologeticus*. He assured the Romans that Christians "are always praying for all emperors, for . . . a safe dynasty, brave armies, a faithful Senate, and a quiet world.". . .
A year later, passing with strange celerity from persuasive
defense to ferocious attack, he issued *De Spectaculis*, a scorn-
ful description of the Roman theaters as citadels of obscen-
ity, and of the amphitheaters as the acme [pinnacle] of man's
inhumanity to man. And he concluded with a bitter threat:

> Other spectacles will come—that last eternal Day of Judg-
> ment . . . when all this old world and its generations shall be
> consumed in one fire. How vast the spectacle will be on that
> day! How I shall marvel, laugh, rejoice, and exult, seeing so
> many kings—supposedly received into heaven—groaning in
> the depths of darkness!—and the magistrates who persecuted
> the name of Jesus melting in fiercer flames than they ever
> kindled . . . against the Christians!—sages and philosophers
> blushing before their disciples as they blaze together! . . . and
> tragic actors now more than ever vocal in their own tragedy,
> and players lither of limb by far in the fire, and charioteers
> burning red on the wheel of flame!

Such unhealthy intensity of imagination does not make for orthodoxy. As Tertullian aged, the same energy that in his youth had courted pleasure now turned into a fierce denunciation of every consolation but those of faith and hope. He addressed woman in the coarsest terms as "the gate by which the demon enters," and told her that "it is on your account that Jesus Christ died.". . . . Sinking into a morose puritanism, Tertullian in his fifty-eighth year rejected the orthodox Church as too sullied with worldly ways. . . . He condemned all Christians who became soldiers, artists, or state officials; all parents who did not veil their daughters; all bishops who restored repentant sinners to communion; finally he called the pope *pastor moechorum*—"shepherd of adulterers."

Origen: A Prolific Writer

Despite him the Church prospered in Africa. Able and devoted bishops like Cyprian made the diocese of Carthage almost as rich and influential as Rome's. In Egypt the growth of the Church was slower, and its early stages are lost to history; suddenly, late in the second century, we hear of a "Catechetical School" in Alexandria, which wedded Christianity to Greek philosophy, and produced two major fathers of the Church. Both Clement and Origen were well versed in pagan literature, and loved it after their own fashion; if their spirit had prevailed there would have been a less destructive break between classical culture and Christianity.

When Origenes Adamantius was seventeen (202) his father was arrested as a Christian, and condemned to death. The boy wished to join him in prison and martyrdom; his mother, failing to deter him by other means, hid all his clothes. Origen sent his father letters of encouragement: "Take heed," he bade him, "not to change your mind on our account." The father was beheaded, and the youth was left to care for the mother and six young children. Inspired to greater piety by the many martyrdoms he saw, he adopted the ascetic life. He fasted much, slept little and on bare ground, wore no shoes, and subjected himself to cold and nakedness; finally, in rigorous interpretation of Matthew XIX, 12, he emasculated himself. In 203 he succeeded

Clement as head of the Catechetical School. Though he was only eighteen, his learning and eloquence drew many students, pagan as well as Christian, and his fame spread

---

Athenagoras's Plea for Equality

The following is an excerpt from an apology titled Plea for the Christians, *dated to circa 176–180. The author, Athenagoras, a Greek Christian writer, asks that the authorities investigate the truth of anti-Christian rumors before passing judgment and then extend to Christians the same legal protections enjoyed by Roman pagans.*

It is not in accord with your justice that, when others are charged with crimes they are not punished till they are convicted, but in our case the name bears more weight than the evidence at the trial, at which the judges, instead of inquiring whether the accused has committed any wrong, insult the name, as if that were itself a crime. . . . Therefore what is conceded equally to all we claim for ourselves, that we shall not be hated and punished because we are called Christians (for what bearing has the name on evil-doing?), but shall be tried on any charges anyone may bring against us, and either be released on our disproving the charges, or punished if convicted of wickedness—not for the name (for no Christian is a bad man unless he falsely profess our doctrines) but for the wrong done. . . .

Three charges are alleged against us: atheism, cannibalistic banquets, incestuous unions. But if these charges are true, spare no class; proceed at once against the crimes; kill us root and branch, with our wives and children, if any Christian is found to live like the beasts. . . . But if these things are only gossip mongering and empty slanders . . . it is left for you to make inquiry concerning our life, our beliefs, our loyalty and obedience to you, your house, and the monarchy, and thus at length to accord to us nothing more than to those who persecute us.

Naphtali Lewis and Meyer Reinhold, eds., *Roman Civilization, Sourcebook 2: The Empire.* New York: Harper and Row, 1966, p. 586.

throughout the Christian world.

Some ancients reckoned his "books" at 6000; many, of course, were brief brochures; even so Jerome asked, "Which of us can read all that he has written?" In love with the Bible, which through boyhood memorizing had become part of his mind, Origen spent twenty years, and employed a corps of stenographers and copyists, collating in parallel columns the Hebrew text of the Old Testament, a Greek transliteration of that text, and Greek translations of it. . . . Insatiate, he added commentaries, sometimes of great length, on every book in the Bible. In *Peri archon*, "First Principles," he achieved the first orderly and philosophical exposition of Christian doctrine. In a "Miscellany" (*Stromateis*) he undertook to demonstrate all Christian dogmas from the writings of the pagan philosophers. . . . The literal meaning of Scripture, argued Origen, overlay two deeper layers of meaning— the moral and the spiritual—to which only the esoteric and educated few could penetrate. He questioned the truth of Genesis as literally understood: he explained away as symbols the unpleasant aspects of Yahveh's [God's] dealings with Israel; and he dismissed as legends such stories as that of Satan taking Jesus up to a high mountain and offering him the kingdoms of the world. Sometimes, he suggested, scriptural narratives were invented in order to convey some spiritual truth. "What man of sense," he asked,

> will suppose that the first and the second and the third day, and the evening and the morning, existed without a sun or moon or stars? Who is so foolish as to believe that God, like a husbandman, planted a garden in Eden, and placed in it a tree of life . . . so that one who tasted of the fruit obtained life?

A Nobler Way of Life?

. . . God, in Origen, is not Yahveh, he is the First Principle of all things. Christ is not the human figure described in the New Testament, he is the Logos or Reason who organizes the world; as such he was created by God the Father, and is subordinate to him. In Origen . . . the soul passes through a succession of stages and embodiments before entering the body; and after death it will pass through a like succession before arriving at God. Even the purest souls will suffer for a while in Purgatory; but in the end all souls will be saved. After the "final conflagration" there will be another world with its long history, and then another, and another. . . . Each will improve on the preceding, and the whole vast sequence will slowly work out the design of God.

We cannot wonder that Demetrius, Bishop of Alexandria, looked with some doubt upon the brilliant philosopher who adorned his diocese and corresponded with emperors. He refused to ordain Origen to the priesthood, on the ground that emasculation disqualified him. But while Origen was traveling in the Near East two Palestinian bishops ordained him. Demetrius protested that this infringed his rights; he convened a synod of his clergy; it annulled Origen's ordination, and banished him from Alexandria. Origen removed to Caesarea, and continued his work as a teacher. There he wrote his famous defense of Christianity *Contra Celsum* [a rebuttal to an attack on Christianity made by a pagan named Celsus]. With magnanimous spirit he admitted the force of Celsus' arguments; but he replied that for every difficulty and improbability in Christian doctrine there were worse incredibilities in paganism. He concluded not that both were absurd, but that the Christian faith offered a nobler way of life than could possibly come from a dying and idolatrous creed.

Christianity Becomes a Philosophy

In 250 the Decian persecution [i.e., that launched by the emperor Decius] reached Caesarea. Origen, now sixty-five, was arrested, stretched on the rack, loaded with chains and an iron collar, and kept in prison for many days. But death caught up with Decius first, and Origen was released. He lived only three years more; torture had fatally injured a body already weakened by unremitting asceticism. He died as poor as when he had begun to teach, and the most famous Christian of his time. As his heresies ceased to be the secret of a few scholars, the Church found it necessary to disown him; Pope Anastasius condemned his "blasphemous opinions" in 400, and in 553 the Council of Constantinople pronounced him anathema. Nevertheless, nearly every later Christian savant for centuries learned from him, and depended upon his work; and his defense of Christianity impressed pagan thinkers as no "apology" had done before him. With him Christianity ceased to be only a comforting faith; it became a full-fledged philosophy, buttressed with Scripture but proudly resting on reason.

Roman Persecution of the Christians

Robert Payne

The Romans wanted to eliminate Christianity in the Empire. To discourage the new faith, the Roman authorities launched a series of periodic and often brutal persecutions against the Christians. Following is Robert Payne's graphic and dramatic summary of these persecutions, which lasted from the mid–first century to the opening of the third. Payne was a journalist, translator, world traveler, historian, and prolific author of more than fifty books, including the widely read *Gold of Troy* and *Ancient Greece*.

"The blood of the martyrs is the seed of the Church," wrote Tertullian of Carthage, and in the long history of Christianity the blood was continually being spilt and the seed was continually flowering.

From the beginning Christianity was pitted against the massive power of the Roman Empire ruling by armed might with fearful weapons of coercion. There was no thought of compromise. If a conquered nation rebelled or a religious sect continued to exist against the will of the Romans, the punishment was extermination. But the Christians, living quietly and obscurely, cultivating their religion behind closed doors, outwardly no different from the other laboring folk except perhaps that they were more tranquil, gentle, and modest, did not at first attract very much attention to themselves. Christianity was still a secret mystery with its mysterious passwords which the faithful drew in the air or in the dust in order to recognize one another: the ship, the ark, the

Excerpted from Robert Payne, *The Christian Centuries: From Christ to Dante* (New York: Norton, 1966). Copyright ©1966 by Robert Payne.

anchor, the dove, the fish. . . . The chief characteristics of the Christians were patience and a quiet faith.

The Earliest Martyrs

The first Christians to be martyred died at the orders of Nero [reigned 51–68]. "Nero first bled the infant Church," wrote the Church historian Eusebius. "Then it was that Peter had his loins girded by another than himself, and both he and Paul were condemned as atheists." Tertullian claimed that Peter "suffered a passion like that of the Saviour and Paul obtained the same coronation as John the Baptist." Legend has embroidered on the manner of their deaths, and in the apocryphal *Acts of Peter* we hear how Peter was arrested, brought before the Prefect Agrippa, and sentenced to be crucified. He asked to be crucified with his head downward, and in this position delivered a sermon to the crowd, saying that he was following the command of Christ that everything be turned upside down. The apocryphal *Acts of Paul* describes an even stranger death, for it tells how Nero in a rage because Paul had converted a favorite cupbearer to Christianity ordered him to be beheaded "in accordance with the Roman law." Paul was taken to the place of execution:

> Then turning toward the east, Paul lifted up his hands to heaven and prayed much; and after having conversed in He-brew with the fathers during prayer, he bent his neck and spoke no more. When the lictor cut off his head, milk splashed on the dress of a soldier. And the soldier, and all who stood nearby, were astonished at this sight and glorified God, who had thus honored Paul. And they went away and reported everything to Caesar. (*Acts of Paul*, 5)

The executions of Peter and Paul during the last tumultuous years of Nero's reign went unrecorded by the Roman historians. Suetonius mentions the persecutions of the Christians casually, as though it were something well-known, inevitable, and perhaps scarcely worth mentioning. When the great fire of Rome broke out on July 19, A.D. 64, Nero was staying with the veterans of the praetorian guard in Antium, but hurried back in time to admire the blaze. The fire raged unchecked for five days, and Suetonius tells us that the emperor's household servants were seen fanning the flames. "To quieten the rumors," says Tacitus, "Nero placed the blame on the Christians and inflicted the most exquisite tortures on these people who were hated for their abominations.". . .

The sullen rage of Nero took many forms, and no one was ever able to count his private and public murders. The massacre of the Christians, like so many of his massacres, seems to have been an afterthought. The strange power of the Christians was already being felt, and their doctrines were known. Among the beliefs of the early Christians was the Second Coming of Christ, which would be attended by fire storms, the whole earth becoming a single searing flame; and it is possible that Nero believed or was convinced that the Christians had deliberately fired the city to fulfill the prophecy. The punishment reserved for the Christians depended upon the whims of Nero. Later it would assume a more formal and familiar character.

The Death of Polycarp

Four years later Nero killed himself, having committed so many atrocities that wherever he turned he found himself confronting avengers. Thereafter, for twenty-seven years, the Christians were left in peace. By A.D. 95 the Church was sufficiently powerful to demand the attentions of the government. . . .

Bishop Polycarp of Smyrna showed a gentler temper, and embraced martyrdom hesitantly. At the annual games given by Philip of Tralles . . . the pagans in order to punish the growing influence of the Church had called for the martyrdom of eleven Christians who were to be given over to the wild beasts. They demanded that the aged bishop, who had once sat at the feet of St. John, should also be executed. Three days passed before the police caught up with Polycarp in a cottage outside the city. It was evening when they reached the cottage, and he could have escaped under cover of darkness. Instead, he calmly offered food and drink to his captors and asked to be allowed to pray for a while, and then accompanied them to the city, where he was met by the captain of police, who asked: "What is the harm of saying 'Caesar is Lord,' and offering incense?" This simple formula in honor of the imperial cult had been devised to ensure that no Christians should escape from the net. By confessing that "Caesar is Lord," the Christians were compelled to accept that all sovereignty came from the emperor. Polycarp refused to obey, and was hurried to the arena. It was Sunday morning, and the crowds were waiting.

The governor of Smyrna, Titus Statius Quadratus, was present, and he seems to have hoped that at the last moment the old bishop would see the error of his ways. "Have respect for your age," he said. "Swear by the Fortune of Caesar, repent, and say 'Away with the atheists!'" The old man sighed, raised his eyes to heaven, waved in the direction of the crowds huddled in the arena, and said: "Away with the atheists!" In this way, ironically, he accepted the challenge of the governor.

"Swear, and I will set you free. Revile Christ!" the governor went on, and Polycarp answered: "I have served Him for eighty-six years, and He has done me no wrong. How can I speak evil of my King, who saved me?"

The governor tried again, begging him to reconsider his decision, but all Polycarp would say was: "I am a Christian! If you wish to learn what it is to be a Christian, you would have to listen to me for a whole day."

The governor said, "It is the people you must convince," and Polycarp answered, "I could reason with you, for we have been taught to give Caesar his due, but I do not believe the people are worthy to hear any defense from me."

"Then I will have to throw you to the wild beasts unless you repent."

"Bring them in! Repentance from the better to the worse is no change to be desired, but it is good to change from cruelty to justice.". . .

When it became clear that Polycarp . . . would continue in his ways, the herald was sent out to proclaim his sentence of death. He was taken to the stake, and when they were about to nail him to it, he said: "Leave me as I am, for He who enables me to abide the fire will also enable me to abide unflinching at the stake." Then he prayed, and the fire was lit. As he stood there, stripped naked, he resembled, says Marcion, "a loaf in the oven," a loaf that refused to burn, for the flames arched over him like a ship's sail, and he was untouched until the *confector* stabbed him; then he fell, and the flames consumed him. "Later," wrote Marcion, "we gathered up his bones, which were more valuable than jewels or gold, and we laid them in a safe place."

Beheaded and Mauled by Lions

There is no very good reason to distrust these accounts of the early martyrs. Their replies to their inquisitors ring true. It was an age when shorthand was well-known and abundantly practiced, and the trial and testimony of the martyrs would quite naturally be preserved with their relics. The proper bureaucratic procedures were invoked; certificates were issued to those who abjured Christ, and reports on the executions were no doubt drawn up and kept in voluminous files. Persecutions however were intermittent. A governor with an eye for promotion would promote the imperial cult and punish all offenders, while another like Pliny the Younger, sent to govern Bithynia by the Emperor Trajan, would show a marked distaste for ordering the execution of inoffensive maid-servants who had embraced the Christian faith. Only in Rome does the cry, *"Christianos ad leones,"* ["throw the Christians to the lions"] seem to have been heard continually. For the Roman mobs the Christians performed the same service as the gladiators: their deaths provided entertainment.

The practices of the inquisitors differed widely, according to their moods and the determination of the Christians to offer themselves up for martyrdom. *The Acts of the Scillitan Saints*, the earliest surviving document concerning Christian martyrs in Africa, dated July 17, A.D. 180, shows a governor earnestly pleading with the Christians to renounce their faith and offering them thirty days in which to reconsider their errors. The mood is tranquil and restrained. Ultimately the Christians refuse to renounce their faith and walk cheerfully to the execution ground. There is no torture. They are beheaded or stabbed to death.

About the same time the Christians in Lyons and Vienne were being hideously tortured. *The Letter from the Churches of Lyons and Vienne,* attributed to St. Irenaeus, describes a scene not unlike a concentration camp in Germany. Torture assumed a peculiarly modern form. It was not enough that prisoners should be flogged, then mauled by wild beasts, then roasted on an iron chair, but they must be submitted to every degradation that the imagination of the Roman prosecutors could evolve. The aim was not only to destroy the Christian physically, but in the process to destroy him spiritually as well, to reduce him to a state of screaming nothingness. Relays of torturers worked on the prisoners from morning to night; the torturers themselves were tortured by their long hours and the terrible conditions under which they worked; and the prisoners, exhausted beyond endurance and scarcely knowing what they were saying, sometimes disavowed their beliefs only to learn that apostasy offered them no advantages. Denied a public martyrdom, they were sometimes suffocated to death in their cells. Then their bodies were thrown to the dogs.

The Letter from the Churches of Lyons and Vienne is a terrifying document which could only have been written by a man who had seen these tortures at close hand. The heart trembles and the pen races as he describes with jagged nerves the outrages committed on the innocent. One torture follows another, one nightmare follows another, and the accumulative effect is to suggest that Roman officialdom suffered from a failure of nerve, a blind nihilism. . . .

"I Will Not Serve"

In fact, it was among the "good" Roman emperors [those that ruled from about 100 to 180] that some of the greatest excesses were committed against the Christians. The Antonine emperors, scrupulously observing the letter of the law, permitted the greatest massacres. Commodus [180–192], the degenerate son of Marcus Aurelius and one of the very worst emperors, proved to be one of the most tolerant to the Christians, being influenced by his Christian concubine and other Christians who flocked to his court. He is known to have given pardons to those under arrest and to have relaxed the rigid laws of summary persecution. With the death of Commodus and the rise to power of Septimius Severus

---

The Martyrdom of Blandina

This tract, describing the horrific death of a Christian woman during a persecution that took place under Marcus Aurelius (reigned 161–180), is taken from an account written by one of the survivors.

Finally . . . on the last day of the gladiatorial combats, Blandina was again brought in, together with Ponticus, a boy of about fifteen, and they had been brought in daily to witness the torture of the others, and attempts were made to force them to swear by the very idols, and because they remained steadfast and regarded them as nothing, the mob was roused to fury so that they had neither pity for the youth of the boy nor respect for the feminine sex, and they exposed them to all the horrors and led them in turn through every torture, repeatedly trying to force them to swear but being unable to do this. For Ponticus was encouraged by his sister, so that even the heathen saw that she was urging him on and encouraging him, and after he had nobly endured every torture he gave up the ghost. But the blessed Blandina, last of all, like a noble mother who has encouraged her children and sent them forth triumphant to the king, herself also enduring all the conflicts of the children, hastened to them, rejoicing and glad at her departure, as if called to a marriage feast and not being thrown to the beasts. And after the scourging, after the wild beasts, after the roasting seat, she finally was placed in a net and thrown to a bull. She was tossed about for some time by the animal but was insensitive to what was happening to her because of her hope and hold upon what had been entrusted to her and her communion with Christ. And she also was sacrificed, and the heathen themselves confessed that never had a woman among them suffered so many and such horrible tortures.

Leon Bernard and Theodore B. Hodges, eds., *Readings in European History.* New York: Macmillan, 1958, p. 34.

[193–211], a new era of total persecution began. Septimius Severus was a "good emperor," capable and efficient, intolerant of any power but his own; and the Christians, who had lived tolerably under Commodus, were now hunted down like wild beasts. One emperor would be tolerant, the next intolerant. So it happened that the weak Alexander Severus [222–235], who is said to have worshiped Christ together with the pagan gods in his private chapel, was followed by the ruthless Maximin [235–238], who issued orders to renew the persecution. His example was followed by Decius [249–251] under whom the Christians suffered as they had never suffered before.

Confronted with the threatened total collapse of the empire, Decius acted with great firmness. He declared total war on the Christians, regarding them as wanton destroyers of the empire, a fifth column sapping at the energies of the empire from within. He was incensed, like other emperors before him, by their exclusivity, their refusal to worship him, to bear arms, or to obey the orders of their governors. "*Non serviam*" (I will not serve), a cry that was to go down the ages, was heard often during that terrible reign. Where Decius excelled, and where other emperors had failed, was in his determination to carry out his threats. Persecution in the past was sporadic, unorganized, inefficient. Decius was the first to organize the mass slaughter of Christians.

The Great Persecution

The Christians fought back; they were in no mood to assent to their own extermination. We hear of armed groups of Christians rescuing prisoners destined for martyrdom, killing the guards, fleeing by night to some stronghold where they could defend themselves. There are no records of an organized Christian militia, but it is clear that a loosely organized militia existed. The Decian persecution lasted for three years, from A.D. 249 to A.D. 251. With the death of Decius the persecutions were abandoned, not to be resumed until the closing years of the reign of Diocletian [284–305] half a century later. Then once more there was a brief period when the Church confronted the full weight of the terror.

Like Decius, Diocletian was a frontier general, concerned above everything else to preserve the might of the army and the authority of his government [although he was goaded into action largely by his coemperor, Galerius]. There opened on February 23, A.D. 303, the large-scale massacre that the Christians called "the Great Persecution." Uncounted thousands were executed for refusing to drop incense into the burners erected on the altars dedicated to the emperor. We hear of executioners who dragged their victims to the altar and made them drop the incense by main force, and sometimes they would fill dead hands with incense and then cast it on the sacrificial flames. In this way the commands of the imperial edict were obeyed.

The Coming of Constantine

"The Great Persecution" ended abruptly when Diocletian renounced the throne and retired into the immeasurable solitudes of his great palace at Spalato on the Dalmatian coast. At the time, Diocletian was the emperor of the East and Maximian the emperor of the West. By agreement they decided to retire at the same time, leaving the thrones of the empire to Galerius and Constantius Chlorus, the one a ruthless Thracian general concerned only with the army and the aggrandizement of his own person, the other a Roman nobleman tolerant and gentle in his dealings with his subjects. "He was a good and kindly man who strove to improve the fortunes of provinces and individuals and was indifferent to enriching the treasury," wrote Eutropius of Constantius Chlorus. "He liked to say that it was better for wealth to be in the hands of individuals than stored in a guard-house." Galerius ruled the East, continuing to persecute Christians. Indeed, he had been the instigator of "the Great Persecution" and the chief agent of its success. Constantius Chlorus contented himself with burning down a few churches as a token of his determination to root out a dangerous sect. He was the ruler of the West, his empire stretching across Britain, Spain, and France, and all of Italy. He died in Britain in York in A.D. 306, and his soldiers promptly elected his son Constantine to the purple. At that moment the long awaited turning-point in the fortunes of Christianity took place. . . .

Handsome, arrogant, efficient, in love with power and his own glory, Constantine was to give an ineffaceable shape to Christianity. He gave it earthly power, wealth, and official sanction. From being persecuted, the Christians became rulers. The most dangerous of gifts was granted to them— official protection.

Rival Religions Compete With and Influence Christianity

Stewart Perowne

One formidable problem the early Christians encountered was competition with popular pagan belief systems, especially the mystery cults from the eastern Mediterranean and Near Eastern spheres. ("Mystery" referred to the secret initiation rites that were a common feature of such faiths.) The most prominent of these cults were those of Cybele, Mithras, and Isis. In this essay, excerpted from his book *Caesars and Saints: The Rise of the Christian State*, archaeologist and classical historian Stewart Perowne describes the allure of these rival religions to residents of the Empire. He also points out how the beliefs and customs of these faiths subtly influenced Christian thought and practice.

The triumph of Christianity in the early years of the fourth century has for long been regarded as the outcome of a straight fight between paganism and the Faith. In fact, the process was far more subtle, far more complex, the final stage in an evolution during which Christianity was to profit doubly, from its reactions to heresies within, and from its contests with rivals without, by whom the heretics were often influenced.

To start with, there was no such thing as "paganism", as a creed. The word can be used in a negative sense only, to indicate what a man did not believe, not what he did. In fact the word pagan means simply one who lives in a village, just as the word heathen means one who dwells on a heath; that is, remote from civilization, at a time when that had been assimilated to the Christian Church.

A Host of New Religions

To put the growth of Christianity in its right setting and perspective it is necessary to go back to Alexander the Great. His ultimate aim had been the creation of a multi-racial society, and despite his early death, he had gone a long way towards achieving it. His marriage, and that of so many of his soldiers, with Persian brides was a literal allegory of the union of Greek and Persian which he hoped to bring about. The process was carried farther by his successors, the Seleucids and the Ptolemies. These two Greek dynasties ruled in Syria and Egypt respectively, and thereby brought about a fusion of Hellenic [Greek] with Syrian and Egyptian ideas which was of the greatest importance for mankind. The achievement is not easy for a modern mind to grasp. We live in an age of almost feverish physical development, the bewildered heirs of the powers bequeathed to us, in dazzling accumulation, by steam, by electricity, by the internal combustion engine, by nuclear energy. In the physical domain, the post-Alexandrine age knew no such activity. It was utterly stagnant. The only motive power that man knew was the one he had always known, the muscles of his kind and of certain animals, supplemented on the sea by the winds. The only chemical agent was fire. There had been no technological development for centuries. Opposed to this technical inertia, the spiritual vigour of the age is all the more striking. It represented what would be called in the scientific jargon of today "a major break-through". Hitherto, religions had been national. Jahweh [the Hebrew God] was a national god; Rimmon [a Semitic storm god] was another, Dagon [a Philistine god] a third. Assyria had its gods, and Egypt had yet others.

The Alexandrine system did away with this narrow religious nationalism for ever. Henceforth religion was to know no frontiers, no nationality. This idea, which sounds so modern, so "Christian", in fact antedates Christianity by three centuries.

Once the barriers were down, the Mediterranean world was flooded by a host of new cults, and all of them came from the east. They may be divided into three main classes, geographically. First there were the religions of Asia Minor. That is only natural. Asia Minor had been "Greek" for centuries; but it was also the heir, political and spiritual, of Persia. The very countryside, with its lush meadows and perennial streams nestling between the great, gaunt uplands and the blue sea, is quite unlike that of Hellas [Greece]. Next came the deities of Egypt, tailored by the Ptolemies for western society. Third and finally were the gods of Syria. Could, then, the west produce no new faith of its own? Yes, one: and that was an eastern importation, too. The cult of the deified emperors, which was to become the official religion of Rome, was modelled on the divine honours paid by oriental subjects to their sovereigns: it was even in the eastern parts of the empire that it received its first manifestations, so paramount had the east become in the realm of the spirit.

Cybele, the Great Mother

The Asian cults reached Rome during the Punic Wars [the three wars Rome fought with Carthage between 264 and 146 BC]. The Sybil had promised that the Great Mother, Cybele, would bring victory to the Romans against the defeated but still formidable Hannibal who had sought asylum in Asia. In the form of a black aerolith, kindly supplied by king Attalus, she made a formal entry into Rome, where many of the first families, remembering their Trojan origin, were delighted to do her honour. In the same year, 202, Scipio defeated Hannibal at Zama. Cybele had arrived, soon to be followed by her consort, Attis. These deities, originally Thracian, were celebrated by ceremonies which included frenzied "possession" culminating in self-castration. The cult, despite its un-Roman nature, flourished at Rome, as did later importations from the same source. It was to their votaries [adherents] that the word "fanatic" was first applied; but they appealed to the emotions, and they stayed on. The death and resurrection of Attis, represented by a decorated tree rather like our Christmas trees, was commemorated hard by the imperial palace itself, and the cult of Cybele, the Great Mother, spread to Spain, Britain, Africa and Gaul. The image of the goddess was transported on a chariot, amid the acclamations of the faithful, in a manner which seems to prefigure the veneration paid to the statue of Our Lady in the streets of contemporary Seville during Holy Week. In both cases, the processions enjoy official patronage. It was, moreover, from the cult of Cybele that the adherents of Mithras were to borrow the disgusting ceremony of the *taurobolium*, or baptism in the blood of a slaughtered bull, the neophyte cringing in a pit wherein, through perforated boards, he was drenched by the steaming blood of the victim.

Sarapis and Isis

The Egyptian contribution to international religion was very different in origin and expression. The first Ptolemy realized two things: first, that the traditional religion of Egypt, ancient and august as it was, would not appeal to his Greek subjects, secondly, that the overwhelming prestige of the ancestral cults must nevertheless be exploited. Hence came into being the synthetic cult of Sarapis. Sarapis himself is of uncertain origin: perhaps he came from Sinope, on the Black Sea coast of Asia Minor, perhaps from Babylon; but the name seems to be undoubtedly derived from *Osiris-Apis* (Usur-api) the protective deity of the Memphis necropolis. The great statue in the Sarapeum in Alexandria, the mother-church of the cult, was . . . one of the last expressions of the Greek genius for representing godhead, recalling as it did, in the features of the deity, his double character of ruler of the abundant earth, and monarch of the kingdom of the dead. With Sarapis was associated Isis, the sister-wife of Osiris, and Horus, their son. Of this triad, it was Isis who attracted the greatest multitude of votaries. Both Isis and Sarapis were early installed in Rome, and throughout the Mediterranean. Their appeal was twofold: the magnificence of the ritual of their ceremonies, and the sense of certainty they bestowed. The former was to influence even the practice of the Catholic Church. When the veneration of the Virgin as the Theotokos, or Mother of God, was introduced (about . . .

391) devotees of Isis were able to continue their worship of the mother-goddess merely by changing her name. In many cases the statues of Isis served as those of her successor-deity. The practice of suspending . . . representations of various parts of the human body, in gratitude for cures, the ceremonial burning of candles, even the monastic tonsure [shaved patch on the head] may all have been taken over from the earlier faith. The peace of mind which the Sarapis religion bestowed was its second outstanding advocate. Alexandria was a hotbed of "philosophy", just as Athens and many another hellenized city were later to become. Men and women argued endlessly "about it and about": Sarapis promised endless felicity. No wonder therefore that his religion became so widely popular. In Rome, it was soon to enjoy court favour. The Flavians, the Antonines, the Severans [dynasties of Roman emperors, in the late first, second, and early third centuries, respectively] all patronized it. The arch-hellenist, Hadrian, constructed a Sarapeum [altar to Sarapis] in his great "villa" at Tibur which to this day remains one of its most imposing features. In the empire the Egyptian religion reached its apogee at the beginning of the third century AD. Thereafter, it yielded the primacy to the religions of Syria, and to the Persian Mithras.

Persian Influences

This was partly due to the patronage of the Semitic Severans, and their connexion with the sun god of Homs. But even without this official favour the Syrian religions would have won adherents. In fact, they had been doing so for some time. They spread all over the empire. In Italy, in Spain, even in Britain inscriptions have come to light honouring the gods of Syria. Generally speaking, the Syrian deities were connected with the sun, or were regarded as being one with it. Thus, they were well on the road to monotheism. They had another advantage: they made a serious attempt to work out a systematic and scientific theology. This they owed to the Persians. It was Persian astronomers who had plotted the courses of the stars, and who had established that certain stars returned to certain portions of the heavens at regular intervals. They were undimmed, timeless. Therefore, *a fortiori* [logically speaking], must not the power who had made them be omnipotent and eternal? These speculations had a profound effect on religion, even on Judaism itself. Before the Captivity, the Jews believed in a *sheol*, or underworld, as gloomy and feeble as that of Homer. But Judaism returned from "beyond the river" with a sense of heaven, a place of bliss beyond the stars—a projection of the afterlife which became almost universally adopted by every religion, and has lasted in popular imagery down to our own age. It came from Persia. In [one historian's] words: "Chaldaean astrology, of which the Syrian priests were the convinced disciples, had supplied them with the elements of a scientific theology. It had led them to the idea of a god enthroned far away from the earth, above the zone of the stars, almighty, universal and eternal, everything here below being regulated by the revolutions of the heavens during infinite cycles of years, and it had at the same time taught them to adore the sun, the radiant source of earthly life and of human reason."

In its final form, therefore, Roman religion was a good deal farther removed from the old pieties that Augustus had sought to restore, than it was from Christianity. The rivals were all bent on attaining the same goal—eternal bliss. By isolating the supreme being who dwelt in the distant heavens from the boundaries of a sublunar world, Syro-Persian religion had started on the path which would end in Christian monotheism. Gradually, the religious and mystical spirit of the east was to impose itself on the whole of society. It was this spirit which prepared all nations to unite within the bosom of a single, universal Church.

The Rise of the Papacy

David Nicholas

The early Christian Church suffered from a lack of central leadership. Each Christian community had its presiding bishop, but the bishops often disagreed and were unable, even with the help of the emperors, to achieve unity in doctrinal matters (those matters involving church doctrine, or accepted ideas and rules). The need for a spiritual head of the church eventually led to the rise of the popes in Rome, a process that took several centuries. David Nicholas, an associate professor of history at the University of Nebraska, here provides a thumbnail sketch of that rise, highlighted most in its early years, he says, by the papacy of Leo the Great (bishop of Rome from 440 to 461), who helped to define the papal office more than any other pope before Gregory I (sixth century).

The elevation of the pope, technically the bishop of Rome, to a position of unquestioned primacy in the western church took some seven centuries. The popes were claiming universal dominion by the late fourth century, but they lost effective control of the churches of northern Europe during the confusion of the invasions [of the Germanic "barbarians" in the fifth and sixth centuries]. Although they corresponded with Frankish monarchs and churchmen and were instrumental in the reconversion of Britain to Christianity, they regained their full authority only in the eighth century.

Several conditions furthered the popes' aims. As bishops of the capital city of the empire, they had enormous prestige. The earliest bishops of Rome were men of considerable abil-

Excerpted from *The Medieval West, 400–1450*, by David Nicholas (Homewood, IL: Dorsey Press, 1973). Reprinted by permission of the author.

ity and powers of articulation. They were able to keep their community in existence even in the worst of times, and they corresponded regularly with the leaders of other churches. As the church of Rome became prosperous, its bishops were generous toward needy churches and helped found some communities. They created a series of ecclesiopolitical debts to be repaid. The bishop of Rome was asked to arbitrate some of the controversies over heresy in the fourth century, and his opinion was invariably orthodox. It is no accident that the most important heresies had spent their course by the time the popes began to obtain recognition of their claims of primacy. Orthodoxy of opinion added prestige, particularly in the nonspeculative west.

By far the most important weapon in the pope's spiritual arsenal was the so-called Petrine theory of delegated spiritual authority. Addressing his disciple Simon shortly before

Leo the Great, "Unworthy Heir" to Peter

Leo envisioned the pope in Rome as the spiritual heir to Peter, "the rock" on whom the Church had supposedly been built; therefore the pope held more spiritual authority than other bishops, a concept that has endured to the present. Scholar Tony Lane summarizes Leo's contributions to the papacy.

Leo was bishop of Rome from 440 to 461 and was one of the greatest of the popes—he is often called 'Leo the Great'. He was a formidable person. In 452 he personally persuaded Attila the Hun to turn back from attacking Rome. Three years later, when the Vandals did take Rome, he managed to check the destruction and killing. Leo is famous especially for his teaching on the person of Jesus Christ and the Roman papacy. His teaching on Jesus Christ is found especially in his *Tome*, written in refutation of the heretic Eutyches. . . .

Leo is also famous for his teaching on the Roman papacy. The claims of Rome began to be heightened in the second half of the fourth century. Leo drew together the teaching of his predecessors and made of it a coherent whole—falling not far

the crucifixion, Jesus said (Matthew 16:18-9) "Thou art Peter, and upon this rock I will build my church . . . and I will give unto thee the keys of the kingdom of heaven; and whatsoever thou shalt bind on earth shall be bound in heaven, and whatsoever thou shalt loose on earth shall be loosed in heaven." While the Protestant interpretation of this passage was to hold that the "peter" (rock) to which Jesus was referring was Simon's statement that Jesus was Christ, the son of God, the Roman Catholic view, which was current in the Middle Ages, holds that Simon was the rock upon which Jesus chose to build his church. Since Peter supposedly founded the church of Rome and was martyred there, his successors as bishops of Rome had the "power of the keys," complete spiritual power in the world.

The earliest popes had no real way to put this doctrine into effect, but Pope Damasus I was able to claim primacy in mat-

---

short of present-day papal claims. He saw the Pope as the 'unworthy heir' of Peter. In Roman law, the heir takes the place of the deceased. This means that the pope has, as heir of Peter, inherited all the authority given to Peter by Jesus Christ (Matthew 16:18–19). In a sense it is Peter himself who acts and speaks through the pope. This puts the pope on a different plane from all other bishops. He is far more than merely the first or chief bishop. They all derive their authority from the pope and he can remove them at will. The pope has the responsibility of governing the whole world-wide church.

Leo's claims were never accepted in the East. In the West they received a varying measure of acceptance throughout the Middle Ages. Leo saw the pope as the *unworthy* heir of Peter. The qualification is important. The pope's status is legal and does not depend on his personal holiness or merit. During the Middle Ages and later this distinction has often had to be invoked since the morality of many of the popes has been infamous rather than famous.

Tony Lane, *Exploring Christian Thought*. Nashville: Thomas Nelson and Sons, 1984, pp. 49–50.

ters of faith by the late fourth century. Rivalry increased with the patriarchs of Alexandria and Constantinople, the leading bishops of the eastern empire. The council of Constantinople in 381 stated that the patriarch of Constantinople was supreme in the east, but that he was subordinate to the pope. Damasus I refused to accept even this, on grounds that he obtained his authority from Peter, not from a council. The pontificate of Leo I, the Great (440–61) was crucial. Not only was he, rather than the emperor, the leader of the defense of Rome against the Huns and the Vandals: in 445 the emperor Valentinian III decreed that the pope was supreme over all other bishops in the west and ordered the officials of the state to assist in the enforcement of these claims.

The position of the pope nonetheless remained largely theoretical for some years. The pope could never maintain himself in barbarian Italy without protection of a secular power, but with protection came secular domination. After much of Italy was reconquered by the eastern Roman emperor in the sixth century, the popes were usually of eastern origin and orientation, recognizing the lordship of the emperor but claiming spiritual primacy over the patriarch of Constantinople. Some of the popes, such as Gregory the Great, were comparatively independent, but they lost effective authority in the west until the eighth century, when the Franks rescued them from the Lombards and became masters of the popes themselves.

Chapter 4

The Triumph of Christianity

Turning|Points

IN WORLD HISTORY

Christianity Becomes Rome's Official Religion

W.H.C. Frend

In the short span of a few decades in the mid-to-late fourth century, the Christian Church acquired a persuasive and at times controlling influence over the state and its secular rulers. Christian leaders accomplished this rise in power and influence partly by attacking and curtailing the public worship and religious traditions of non-Christians. One stunning blow to Roman pagans was the removal of the statue of the goddess Victory from its altar in the Roman Senate. Because they believed that the goddess protected the state from harm, pagans considered this an affront to their religious freedom. Another blow to paganism was the emperor Gratian's renunciation of his role as priest of the traditional state religion. The most insulting act of all, in pagan eyes, occurred when the influential bishop Ambrose convinced the emperor Theodosius to recognize Christianity officially and close the pagan temples. As former Cambridge University scholar W.H.C. Frend explains, much of the credit for Christianity's political triumph goes to Ambrose, who relentlessly asserted both his own and the church's authority.

Theodosius had opened his reign in the East with a blast against all the opponents of Nicene truth. Though he was to modify his views in favour of the Eastern interpretation of the Nicene formulae, he never wavered in his conviction

Excerpted from W.H.C. Frend, *The Early Church* (Philadelphia: Lippincott, 1966). Copyright ©1965 by W.H.C. Frend.

that this creed was not only the true faith, but the integrating force which would bind the entire Roman world together. In 380 he had been prepared to use the full power of the State to force Gregory of Nazianze and orthodoxy on the people of Constantinople. In the West, Ambrose of Milan was to provide him with a complete partner both in methods and ideas.

Ambrose is one of those rare historical characters whose claim to fame rests on a single incident, the result perhaps of two or three hours of concentrated thought and dictation, but which was to affect profoundly relationships between Church and State in the Western world for generations to come. . . .

The Rise of Ambrose

He was born in 339, the son of Aurelius Ambrosius, the head of one of the few long-standing Christian families of senatorial rank in Rome who had risen to be praetorian prefect of the Gauls. He died, however, soon afterwards leaving the young Ambrose and his brother in the care of his mother and elder sister. It was a strongly religious household, typified perhaps by the occasion in January 353 when his sister Marcellina received the veil from Pope Liberius and solemnly dedicated her life to virginity. Ambrose's house became the earliest of those Roman patrician palaces devoted to Christian piety and learning, such as were to flourish under the leadership of Jerome and Pelagius a generation later. . . .

In due course Ambrose followed his father into an administrative career, and at the age of thirty-four found himself Governor of the important province of Aemilia-Liguria in which the city of Milan stood. This had been one of the headquarters of the Imperial Government in the West since the time of Constantine. . . . There is no reason to doubt that he was acclaimed Bishop by popular favour. Having passed from neophyte through the various ecclesiastical grades in eight days he was ordained Bishop on 7 December 373. His episcopate lasted until his death on 6 April 397. In these years Ambrose was confronted with four main tasks; first to extinguish the remains of Arianism in the West; secondly, to assert the rights of the Church over against the State,

thirdly, to overthrow the remaining power of the pagan aristocracy, and finally, to condemn the various theological
opinions which were challenging his own ascetic view of the
Christian life. If one adds his . . . moulding of the Christian
liturgy and hymnody in the direction of congregational
singing, one has the picture of a busy and purposeful life.

Arianism in the West, in the form of support for the creed
of Ariminum, was declining fast, but so long as Valentinian I
lived, Ambrose was denied the opportunity of destroying the
remnants. The Emperor, preoccupied with an able offensive-
defensive campaign on the Danube, was staunchly determined
to uphold a policy of toleration for all religions. . . . When he
died on 17 November 375 Ambrose uttered no regrets. . . . It
was not until the autumn of 378 that his chance for action
came. Then, in a sermon on the true Faith he pointed out how
the 'Arian provinces' of the Empire were being devastated by
the Goths, while those under the protection of Gratian [the
new emperor] were safe. . . . Gratian, a kindly but immature
youth of nineteen, had explicitly continued his father's religious policy by granting toleration to all. . . .

In the summer of 379 Ambrose met the Emperor at
Milan, and gained there an ascendancy over Gratian's mind
which lasted until the latter's death four years later. A general anti-heretical law was the first result, and the second was
that in January 380 Gratian wrote to Ambrose asking him to
send him his sermon 'on the Faith' and to come to Trier and
instruct him personally in it. Further triumphs followed. In
the autumn of 380 he had been instrumental in securing the
election of a Catholic cleric to succeed the semi-Arian Gem-
inius in the capital of Illyricum, Sirmium. . . . Meantime, in
September 381 Ambrose browbeat two of the remaining
Arian leaders into an avowal of heresy and secured their de-
position. When he returned to Milan he had achieved a
[powerful] position in the councils of the State. . . . This situation could have lasted a generation, for when Gratian was
treacherously murdered at Lyon on 25 August 383, he was
still only twenty-five. . . .

[In 390] Valentinian II [Gratian's successor in the West,
who had also been dominated by Ambrose, retired to Gaul]

. . . and Theodosius [who had been emperor in the East since 379] took the remainder of the West under his personal control. In a few months he had his first clash with Ambrose. At Callinicum on the Euphrates frontier [in the Near East] a mob had rioted, and at the instigation of their bishop pillaged a synagogue, while in the same area monks had demolished a chapel. . . . Theodosius ordered the bishop to rebuild the synagogue, and those guilty of riot to be punished. Ambrose intervened. In a long letter to his sister he told how he preached before the Emperor. Jews and pagans, he argued, had been guilty of similar acts in Julian's reign, yet no one had punished them. Why should heresy and infidelity be favoured now? And Ambrose made it plain that unless all penalties were withdrawn against the monks he would not celebrate the Eucharist. Theodosius . . . capitulated.

This was ecclesiastical tyranny pushed to preposterous lengths. Ambrose had claimed for the Church the right of veto over the acknowledged duties of the state. Religion came before public order and the way had been cleared for intervention by any clergy in secular affairs if they thought that their interests might be affected. A year and a half later, however, he had right on his side, and this time he used his authority wisely. The people of Thessalonica [a large town in northern Greece] had been guilty of sedition and murdered one of Theodosius's senior officers. The Emperor with refinement of cruelty had the citizens invited to the circus, and when they were there sent in the soldiers to massacre them. In three hours, some 7,000 people, men, women and children had lost their lives.

This terrible deed would have been shocking in any context. This time, however, Ambrose did not rant. In mid-September 390 he sent a secret letter which rightly has been applauded as a masterpiece of firmness and devastating tact. Three paragraphs may be quoted.

> Suffer me, gracious Emperor. You have a zeal for the faith, I own it, you have the fear of God, I confess it; but you have a vehemence of temper, which if soothed may readily be changed into compassion, but if inflamed becomes so violent

that you can scarcely restrain it. If no one will allay it, let no one at least inflame it. To yourself I would willingly trust, for you are wont to exercise self-control, and by your love of mercy to conquer this violence of your nature.

I advise, I entreat, I exhort, I admonish; for I am grieved that you who were an example of singular piety, who stood so high for clemency, who would not suffer even single offenders to be put in jeopardy, should not mourn over the death of so many innocent persons. Successful as you have been in battle, and great in other respects, yet mercy was ever the crown of your actions. The devil has envied you your chief excellence: overcome him, while you still have the means. Add not sin to sin by acting in a manner which has injured so many.

For my part, debtor as I am to your clemency in all other things; grateful as I must ever be for this clemency, which I have found superior to that of many Emperors and equalled only by one, though I have no ground for charging you with contumacy, I have still reason for apprehension: if you purpose being present, I dare not offer the Sacrifice. That which may not be done when the blood of one innocent person has been shed, may it be done where many have been slain? I believe not.

A vital principle in Christian society had been gained. Above the will of the ruler, and reason of State, stood some form of Christian moral order. From now on, no arbitrary destruction of human life by a State could pass unchallenged. In this one act of calculated heroism years of browbeating, pedantry and arrogance were expunged. The West had produced a great ecclesiastical statesman.

Symmachus and the Altar of Victory

Between the two crises Theodosius had been in Rome, and there witnessed the submission to the Christian Faith of more than 600 members of the Roman aristocracy. Here too, the victory proved to be final. Paganism had been dying slowly. By 390 the majority of the provincial middle-classes had probably become as completely Christian . . . as their forebears had been pagan. In the countryside, the last strongholds of the old religions in the Celtic West were being whittled away by the missionary efforts of men such as Martin of Tours in Northern Gaul, or Theodore of Valais in the Swiss valleys. In the provinces even, there was some demand for anti-pagan legislation. . . . In Rome, however, the pagan aristocracy had for the most part held firm to the old religion. As in the great days of the Empire, theirs was a cult of antiquity rather than a creed; a veneration for forms and customs which had preserved the Roman State, and whose

---

Rival Faiths Declared Illegal

The law quoted here was enacted during the reign of Theodosius I, who helped Ambrose exert the church's authority in state affairs. The statute both legitimizes Christian worship and condemns all other forms of religious expression. The Christians, who had once been unfairly persecuted, had now become the persecutors.

It is our desire that all the various nations which are subject to our Clemency and Moderation, should continue in the profession of that religion which was delivered to the Romans by the divine Apostle Peter, as it hath been preserved by faithful tradition; and which is now professed by the Pontiff Damasus and by Peter, Bishop of Alexandria, a man of apostolic holiness. According to the apostolic teaching and the doctrine of the Gospel, let us believe the one deity of the Father, the Son and the Holy Spirit, in equal majesty and in a holy Trinity. We authorize the followers of this law to assume the title of Catholic Christians; but as for the others, since, in our judgement, they are foolish madmen, we decree that they shall be branded with the ignominious name of heretics, and shall not presume to give to their conventicles the name of churches. They will suffer in the first place the chastisement of the divine condemnation, and in the second the punishment which our authority, in accordance with the will of Heaven, shall decide to inflict.

Leon Bernard and Theodore B. Hodges, eds., *Readings in European History.* New York: Macmillan, 1958, p. 37.

disappearance they feared would endanger its survival. They would have agreed with Julian in regarding Christianity as a revolutionary force, and in the person of Quintus Aurelius Symmachus, they found a powerful advocate.

In the last years of his reign Gratian had pursued an anti-pagan policy. At its outset, he had refused the traditional title of Pontifex Maximus. In 381, under Ambrose's influence he issued an instruction to his praetorian prefect forbidding sacrifices. Next year, he ordered the removal of the Statue of Victory, the age-old symbol of Roman religion and Roman might, from the Senate House. At the same time, he instructed that the funds hitherto allocated by the State for the maintenance of the heathen sacrifices and ceremonies in Rome should be confiscated. A protest by the majority of the Senate was brushed aside. After Gratian's murder, however, the pagan party took heart. Famine and discontent in Rome, together with the appointment of Symmachus as prefect of the city, gave them their chance, and in the summer of 384 Symmachus presented a petition on behalf of the Senate at Valentinian's court. The appeal for the restoration of the Statue of Victory was the aristocracy's final appeal to the glory that was Rome's. After pointing to the prosperity of the Roman State under the patronage of the old gods and the value of maintaining ancestral religious customs, Symmachus ended with an historic plea for religious toleration. 'We plead then, for a respite for the gods of our fathers, the gods of our native land. It is right to believe that that which all men worship is The One. We look on the same stars: the same heaven is above us all; the same universe surrounds us. What matters it by what method each of us reaches the truth? We cannot by a single road arrive at so great a secret'.

Church over State

Few nobler words in the cause of man's right to seek God in his own way have been spoken. The final plea on behalf of the religion which had inspired the founding of the Roman Republic and Empire was its most memorable. Ambrose, however, rose to the situation. Using every artifice of traditional eloquence combined with Christian apologetic he implored Valentinian not to be misled by bad advisers, to re-member that the pagans had persecuted the Church even as late as the reign of Julian, and to bear in mind that tradition and custom were not the characteristics of the natural world. There must be change and improvement, change from pagan error to Christianity. Had he stopped there, the de-bate would have been remembered as one of the classics of the ancient world. But Ambrose could not resist the bullying tactics that he had used against the Arians at Aquileia. He threatened. It was an 'affair of religion'. He spoke 'as a bishop'. If Valentinian were to accept the pagan petition, Christ would not accept his gifts. The menace of excommu-nication together with an appeal to the memory of his dead brother, Gratian, carried the day. The petition was dis-missed. Ambrose had gained an ignoble but decisive victory over the old religion. The position of Christianity as the re-ligion of the Latin West was assured. The surrender of the pagan aristocracy to Theodosius in 389 was merely the af-termath of victory.

Ambrose's final years were mainly concerned with contro-verting and condemning opinions which had won support as a reaction against the increasingly ascetic tendency among the leadership of the Western Church. . . . To Ambrose's lik-ing was the condemnation of Bonosus, an Illyrian bishop, guilty of believing that the Virgin Mary after giving birth to Jesus, bore several more children in wedlock with Joseph. Two years later he convened a small council of bishops of Upper Italy to support a papal condemnation of Jerome's ad-versary Jovinian. The latter having become disgusted with monasticism, taught that all baptized persons, whether mar-ried, widows or virgins, had equal respect in regard to their marital state and differed only in respect of their works, and that abstinence was no more pleasing to God than partaking of food with thankfulness. . . .

Ambrose survived the last civil war of Theodosius's reign, the usurpation after the murder of Valentinian II in 392 of the pro-pagan Eugenius. He saw his friend win his final vic-tory on the River Frigidus in September 394 and thereby give the death-blow to pagan hopes. Within a few months

Theodosius had died on 19 January 395, and Ambrose survived him a bare two years. In nearly a quarter of a century
of episcopal government he had taken the Church of Milan
to the peak of authority. Not the Pope but he had over-
thrown Arianism and paganism in the West and had assured
the superiority of Church over State throughout the European Middle Ages. . . . His hymns, if not his translations
from Greek to Latin, became part of the Church's permanent heritage. He was not, however, a wholly attractive character; there was something both of the tyrant and the obscu-
rantist in him, but given the need for a man who combined
the qualities of bishop and statesman on the eve of the fall of
the Western Empire, no better could have been found than
Ambrose of Milan.

How Christian Writers Helped Transform Christianity and Society

Charles Freeman

During the second half of the fourth century, the influential bishop Ambrose and other assertive church leaders brought the Christian faith to a position of spiritual authority over most Roman political and social institutions. Their spiritual successors continued, through their writings and preaching, the transformation of Roman Mediterranean society into a vast Christian community. Among the most influential of these late Roman Christian thinkers were Augustine, Jerome, and John Chrysostom. Their lives, ideas, works, and legacies are ably summarized here by historian Charles Freeman, whom a distinguished colleague recently described as "a man with the enthusiasm, literary skills, and zeal for research which [make] him ideally suited to writing history on a broad scale."

The late fourth and early fifth centuries produced a number of profound thinkers who had been brought up in the traditional world of classical learning, converted to Christianity, and then deployed their penetrating intellects in the service of the church. Of these Augustine was perhaps the most influential. His experiences are detailed in the *Confessions*, a brilliant account of a tortured mind searching for absolute peace. The central chapters of the *Confessions* are concerned with his spiritual experiences in Milan and his eventual con-

Reprinted from *Egypt, Greece, and Rome*, by Charles Freeman (1996), by permission of Oxford University Press. Copyright © Charles Freeman 1996.

version to Christianity. They were written in the late 390s after he had returned to his native Africa. Augustine presents himself as a deeply unworthy man, tormented by his sexuality and harried, although he took some time to recognize the fact, by the looming power of God.

> I broke your lawful bounds and did not escape your lash. For what man can escape it? You were always present, angry and merciful at once, strewing the pangs of bitterness over all my lawless pleasures to lead me on to look for others unallied with pain. You meant me to find them nowhere but in yourself, O Lord, for you teach us by inflicting pain, you smite so you may heal and you kill us so that we may not die away from you.

Augustine came to accept that God's love becomes available to sinners only when they make complete submission to Him. The moment of conversion came after many struggles when he heard the voice of a child asking him to take up the New Testament. He opened it at the words of Paul, 'put on the Lord Jesus Christ and make no provision for the flesh to gratify its desires'. Suddenly he had found his true haven, in the church. Once he had renounced his sexual desires for ever, he was able to be baptized.

After his conversion and baptism, Augustine returned to his native Africa and became bishop of Hippo where he remained until his death thirty years later. While he preferred the life of the monk, he cared deeply about the needs of the ordinary Christians who thronged his churches and was more sensitive than most church leaders to their earthly desires. (He was prepared, for instance, to accept sexuality as an intrinsic part of marriage.) In the remaining years of his life, he applied the brilliance and clarity of his mind to some of the major theological issues of the day. Perhaps the most famous was the dispute with Pelagius, an ascetic who may have been of British birth, over the nature of free will.

Original Sin

Pelagius had argued that each individual had the freedom to follow God's will or not. The hope, of course, was that he or she would choose to aim for a life of perfection, with Christ as the model. In such a case, argued Pelagius, God would support these efforts. Augustine, on the other hand developed a different approach, one that had only been dimly formulated before his time. This was the view that as a result of Adam and Eve's transgressions in the Garden of Eden God had burdened all human beings with an 'original sin' which was passed on from generation to generation. The concept of original sin had never been mentioned by Jesus and Augustine relied on one verse from St Paul (Romans 5:12) for support. The consequences of the sin were, however, profound. Human beings, argued Augustine, were tied by original sin to the earthly pleasures of the world (the evidence was before him in his congregations) and only the grace of God could liberate them from the burden of these pleasures. This grace could be passed on through the sacraments, especially those of baptism and the Eucharist, but it was always a gift from God, not the right of any individual, however good his or her life.

Augustine's God was, therefore, selective. Only a few would be saved. This left uncomfortable questions to be resolved. Was it possible to live a good life and still be deprived of the grace of God? What would happen to those who did not receive this grace or who were never baptized? When challenged by his opponents over what would happen to the souls of babies who had died before they were baptized Augustine was forced to accept that their original sin left them unprotected and they could never be admitted to heaven. Independently Augustine also came to reject Origen's view that eternal punishment was incompatible with the goodness of God and became one of the foremost defenders of a Hell where punishment would be harsh and eternal. There would be no mercy for those to whom the grace of God was not extended.

Augustine's concept of original sin was, in the early fifth century, a minority view held only by some of his fellow bishops in north Africa. As another opponent commented, the whole idea was improbable, making it seem as if the devil, not a loving God, had created man. What was remarkable, however, was that through sheer persistence and intellectual energy Augustine managed to get his view accepted as the official doctrine of the western church after the emperor Honorius insisted the Italian bishops adopt it. The concept of original sin received no support elsewhere. It never travelled to the east (Augustine wrote only in Latin) or was adopted by any other monotheistic religion.

The Right to Deal with Heretics

Augustine attempted to define what was meant by the 'church'. Joining the church and receiving its sacraments presumably increased the chance of receiving the gift of God's grace but the logic of Augustine's views suggested that membership of the church did not guarantee salvation and that those who did not join the church were not necessarily deprived of it. The church, however, had a duty to ensure that all who wished to join and receive the benefits of its sacraments could do so. Augustine's main opponents here were the Donatists (a majority of the Christians in Hippo), who continued to insist that the orthodox church had been fatally damaged during the persecutions and that they were right to keep Christians from joining it. To counter this attack Augustine argued that the validity of the orthodox church did not depend on the worthiness of its members. The sacrament of baptism given by an unworthy priest was still valid in the eyes of God. It followed that the Donatists, through their intransigence, were depriving those who might be eligible for God's grace from receiving it through the sacraments. Therefore it was legitimate to destroy the sect and release its followers to their proper home in the church. This approach reinforced the view taken by Theodosius and Ambrose, that the church, backed by the state, had the right to deal with heresy. Although Augustine cautioned restraint in the methods employed against heretics, his words were used in later centuries to justify the persecutions of medieval and Reformation Europe.

Augustine's Chilling Message

Augustine's last great work, *The City of God*, was prompted by the sack of Rome by the Visigoths in 410. Although the physical damage was not immense (and the Christian Visigoths left the city's churches untouched), the psychological shock certainly was. It seemed as if the world as all had known it was at an end. Much of the book is concerned with pointing out the failure of traditional Roman religion to save the city or provide anything more than a self-glorification of the state. Augustine argued that the true 'city' was, instead, that inhabited by the believers loved by God, a community which extended from earth into heaven. An earthly city, even one so great as Rome, was only a pale reflection of the heavenly one and it was to the heavenly city that the aspirations of men and women must be directed. The fall of Rome was thus of little significance in the eyes of God.

Augustine's influence on the church was profound. His writing and sermons had a clarity and majesty which was unrivalled. His mind penetrated every nook and cranny of Christian thought. Much of his writing, in Book Nine of *The Confessions*, for instance, where his last conversations with his mother are recorded, is deeply moving. He was not a cold intellectual but a human being acutely aware of the power of his emotional feelings. It is hard not to feel some sympathy for him in his agonizing searches for his God. Ultimately, however, his message was a chilling one. There was no salvation without divine grace and this could not necessarily be gained through living a 'good' life. The church had the right to prosecute heretics and call on the state to support it. Only those who are convinced that divine grace is theirs and who through it have liberated themselves from their body's desires can read his works with total ease.

Jerome and the Vulgate Bible

Contemporary with Augustine was another great scholar of the early church, Jerome (*c.* 347–419/20). Jerome was born in the Balkans about 347 of Christian parents but by the age of 12 he was studying philosophy and rhetoric in Rome. He developed a profound love of classical authors and one of the most shattering events of his life was a dream in which God accused him of preferring [the first century B.C. Roman orator and prodigious writer] Cicero to the Bible, for which failing he was flogged. He resolved never to read a pagan author again (though his letters remain full of classical allusions).

Jerome's life was restless and tormented. He travelled incessantly and underwent periods of severe asceticism. In [noted historian] Peter Brown's words, 'The human body remained for Jerome a darkened forest, filled with the roaring of wild beasts, that could be controlled only by rigid codes

Jerome's Dream

In this excerpt from his twenty-second letter, Jerome recounts the dream in which God confronted him and accused him of holding the great Roman pagan writer Cicero in more esteem than the Lord.

Many years ago I had, for the sake of the kingdom of heaven, cut myself off from home, parents, sister, relations and (hardest of all) from the dainty food to which I had become accustomed. I was on my way to Jerusalem to wage my warfare, but I still could not bring myself to part with the library which I had collected with such care and toil at Rome. And so, miserable man that I was, I would fast only that I might afterwards read Cicero. . . . And when at times I returned to my right mind and began . . . to read the prophets, their style seemed rude and repulsive. I failed to see the light with my blinded eyes, but I attributed the fault, not to them but to the sun. . . . Suddenly I was caught up in the spirit and dragged before the judgement seat of the Judge. . . . Asked who and what I was, I replied 'I am a Christian'. 'You lie,' said he who presided, 'You are a Ciceronian, not a Christian. For where your treasure is, there will your heart be also.' Instantly I became dumb and amid the strokes of the lash—for he had ordered me to be whipped—I was tortured even more severely by the fire of conscience . . . I made an oath and called upon his name, saying: 'Lord, if I ever again possess worldly books or read them, I have denied you'. . . . From then on I read the books of God with a zeal greater than I had previously given to the books of men.

F.A. Wright, trans., *Select Letters of St. Jerome*. Cambridge, MA: Harvard University Press, 1963.

of diet and by the strict avoidance of occasions for sexual attraction.' At the same time, however, he studied assiduously and mastered both Greek and Hebrew in addition to his native Latin. It was this breadth of knowledge which recommended him to bishop Damasus of Rome, who employed him first as his secretary (382–4) and then as the translator of the Greek and Hebrew texts of the Old and New Testaments into Latin.

A unified and authoritative translation had long been needed. There were all too many Latin translations of varying quality circulating in the western empire. Jerome faced formidable problems in achieving his task. In Rome his censorious personality and suspicion over a new translation made him so unpopular that after the death of Damasus he was forced to leave the city. The last thirty-four years of his life were spent in Bethlehem [in Palestine] in a monastery and it was here that his translation was finally brought to a conclusion. At first it received little recognition but by the eighth century it was accepted by the church as the authoritative Latin version of the original texts. As the Vulgate (the 'common version') it lasted unchallenged in the Catholic church for centuries and remains one of the great achievements of early Christian scholarship.

The Golden-Mouthed Preacher

The age was also one of great preachers, the most celebrated of whom was John Chrysostom, 'the golden-mouthed' (c. 347–407). In contrast to Augustine and Jerome, John was an easterner, a native of Antioch. From an early age he was such a gifted speaker that it was assumed that he would become a lawyer or civil servant like his father. However, he was baptized when 21 and then took to a life of solitude in the caves around Antioch. He emerged, his health permanently damaged, with a loathing for finery and self-indulgence. Any hint of greed or arrogance aroused his anger and it was said that he would sternly fix his eye on the women in his congregation who appeared overdressed. His harshness was modified, however, by his concern for the poor of his congregations, many of whom welcomed his denunciations of the rich. He was particularly adept at translating his ideas into images which all could grasp.

Until he was 50 John served in Antioch, earning an empire-wide reputation as a preacher. It was during these years that he preached his eight sermons warning Christians against Judaism. These sermons, translated into Latin and transferred to the west, later fuelled anti-Jewish hysteria in medieval Europe. In 398 John was forced to accept the bishopric of Constantinople. It was an unhappy move. He was never at ease in the shadow of an opulent court and made many enemies who exploited his ambivalence towards the worldliness of the empress Eudoxia. He also became caught up in the long-standing rivalry between the sees [bishops] of Alexandria (established long before Constantinople) and Constantinople. Finally he was exiled to a remote village on the coast of the Black Sea where he died in 407.

New Concepts of Spiritual Authority

In 394 the emperor Theodosius had been challenged by a usurper in Gaul, Eugenius. Eugenius was a pagan and attracted the support of many leading Roman senators. Theodosius met their forces at the River Frigidus in the Alps and crushed them. The battle was seen by contemporary Christians as the confirmation of the triumph of their faith. Certainly a different world now existed, with new concepts of spiritual authority and different visions of God and morality. . . . Moreover, a growing preoccupation with the elimination of paganism and heresy meant, inevitably, that the rich diversity of Greco-Roman spiritual experience was stifled, with the result that eventually spiritual aspirations could no longer be expressed outside a specifically Christian context. Jews were increasingly isolated, and the fourth century marks for them, in the words of [scholar] Nicholas de Lange, 'the beginning of a long period of desolation'. The state and church authorities initiated measures to segregate the Jews from mainstream Christian society with consequences that were, in the long term, profound.

The Greek and Roman world had seen a variety of gods whose own relationships and conflicts had often diverted them from human affairs. The single Christian god was portrayed as if He had few other concerns than the behaviour and attitudes of individual human beings. Their sexual behaviour in particular seemed of particular concern to Him. He had supreme majesty and no Christian would have dared to have confronted Him in the confident way a Greek might have done. (Augustine's description of himself in his *Confessions* as 'a mean thing' would have been greeted with incomprehension and, probably, contempt by his Roman predecessors.) It was perhaps at this moment that intense guilt replaced public shame as a conditioner of moral behaviour. Ever more lurid descriptions of the horrors of Hell accompanied the shift. Soon consuming fires and devils with red-hot instruments of torture entered European mythology. There were other aspects of Christian society that were significant. While Christians ensured that the poor were seen as an object of concern (and hence, for the first time, something is known of them), it was also believed that God would be pleased by the magnificence of buildings constructed in His honour. This led inevitably to a tension over the way a Christian society used its resources, whether for the relief of the poor, as the gospels would seem to support, or the glorification of God in gold and mosaic. The collaboration of the state with the only authorized religion has also to be of fundamental importance. These shifts in beliefs helped determine a framework of social, economic, spiritual, and cultural life which has persisted even into the twentieth century. It is certainly arguable that, in this respect, the fourth century is one of the most influential in European history.

The Origin and Spread of Christian Monasteries

C. Harold King

A particularly striking spiritual and social development during the late Roman Empire and early Middle Ages was the monastic movement, composed of devout Christians who showed their devotion to God by withdrawing from everyday life and maintaining a strict, often harsh secluded existence. As historian C. Harold King, formerly of the University of Miami, explains, they chose an ascetic life characterized by austerity and self-denial. Some were hermits who rarely if ever interacted with other people, while others joined monasteries and other group settings.

One of the most interesting aspects of early Christianity is the rise of monasticism. Monasticism means being alone, but being alone for a purpose. The purpose which concerns us was the renunciation of the world and devotion of oneself wholly to religion. Most of our attention will be devoted to the formula most prevalent in the West, the seclusion of devout men and women in monasteries and convents. There were also a few who lived completely alone as hermits. The common factor in both types is the ascetic impulse, the desire to renounce the flesh in order to devote one's whole energy to the life of the spirit.

A Universal Urge

The ascetic impulse has not been limited to Christianity. There were Hindu monks in 2400 B.C., and a sixth century B.C. Hindu monk, Buddha, initiated a new religion in India.

Excerpted from C. Harold King, *A History of Civilization: Earliest Times to the Mid-seventeenth Century*, 2nd ed. (New York: Scribner, 1964).

There were Chaldean Dhaquit monks in 2000 B.C. The Essenes established a Hebrew monastic order near the Dead Sea in the second century B.C. Even among the Greeks, who were dedicated to the satisfactions of this life, there were men such as Pythagoras [who established a monastery-like retreat, dedicated to the study of mathematics, in southern Italy in the sixth century B.C.], capable of the essentials of the ascetic impulse.

It is evident that the ascetic impulse has been found in so many faiths, so many periods, and so many areas, that it amounts to a universal urge. If anyone in modern life has ever thought that his church compromised too much with the world; if anyone has ever felt like withdrawing from a confusion of events that have become too complicated and too distressing, he should be able to appreciate what motivated the early monks. That urgings of the ascetic impulse are common in the nature of us all can be seen from the presence of several books about monasticism on best-seller lists in the twentieth century.

Purity Gives Way to Compromise

The Christian movement was initially a revolt against prevailing values. All who joined this movement were expected to renounce the world. Those feeling its doctrines most strongly spread its tidings to others and a few emulated the suffering of Jesus by their martyrdom. Even though the Church had grown in numbers, however, its membership at the end of the third century held only the strong in faith.

When Christianity was made the official religion of the Empire in the fourth century, the situation changed. Its ranks were swelled by those who found it easier to be Christian now that it was less dangerous and by those who decided that it was expedient to adopt this erstwhile despised doctrine. Renunciation of earthly delights became more difficult and in some respects impossible as the possessors of material wealth and pagan learning swelled the assemblies of the humble. Purity gave way to compromise. Complaints were heard when clergy in magnificent vestments had to be carried in gorgeous litters lest their elegant slippers be contaminated by the common soil of thoroughfares along which the early martyrs had been dragged. The roads were full of "galloping bishops" bent on missions of worldly advantage, and prelates of a church that had come through the fires of persecution now persecuted the men of other faiths. In the same century in which began the reduction of fine points of doctrine to reason by the Fathers, those who could not and would not compromise prepared what has been called "a second chapter in the history of Christian renunciation."

Prodigies of Godliness

The movement that led to both monasticism and eremitism [living as a hermit] began in the East. Eremitism was more popular there, displaying the less attractive aspects of ascetic impulse. Men fled to the most barren places to flagellate [whip] their bodies for the good of their souls. The urge to be alone became a mass hysteria as hundreds rushed to the desert to live sealed off in caves from their fellow men. But it was difficult to find ground not preempted by other hermits or not visited by the curious. Admirers came to view the prodigies of godliness and to catch the miraculous power which emanated from such holy discipline. Cures of persistent diseases were reported. Those who attained the greatest heights of self-torture were most widely famed and such champions bent their efforts to achieve more tortures still.

Most famous of the eastern hermits was St. Simeon Stylites, who existed on a pillar near Antioch for thirty years. On this pillar, where his mortifications of the flesh could be viewed by hundreds of pilgrims, St. Simeon ate only enough to keep alive, refused to bathe, remained standing constantly and when fasting made him too weak to stand alone, was bound to another pillar which acted as a prop.

Although eremitism was the dominant form of asceticism in the East, it was there also that group asceticism began. In Asia Minor Pachomius (292–346) drew together a community of hermits who, though not in communication with one another, abided by the same rules. More ancestral to western monasticism was the community of hermits gathered in Egypt by St. Anthony (251–356), whose regulations were called a *Rule*. This experiment, and another by Paul of Thebes, came to the attention of the West, especially when Jerome and Athanasius (of Nicaean fame) actively promoted monasticism in Rome. In contrast to the East there were some hermits in the West but the favored expression of the ascetic impulse was in group living.

Strictness Tempered by Recognition of Human Limits

Roman organizing genius and sanity were introduced into western monasticism by a Roman noble. St. Benedict (480–543), feeling the call to renounce the world, first became a hermit and inflicted upon himself tortures in true eastern fashion. Then his Roman common sense reasserted itself and he sought a more moderate ascetic life, founding at Monte Cassino the most famous monastery of all time.

Benedict's rule was one of strictness, tempered by intelligent recognition of human limits. Chastity, poverty and obedience were basic vows, although these classic prerequisites did not originate with St. Benedict. What was partly new was the special emphasis on obedience, while still newer was the introduction of the principle of labor because idleness became a sin. The inclusion of reading as a duty had far-reaching importance since monasteries thereafter had reason to collect and preserve books. It is no surprise that a Roman would perceive that labor would exhaust the excess energy of a celibate; that an educated Roman would provide the means by which at least some of the culture of antiquity would be preserved; and that a Roman aristocrat would emphasize unquestioned obedience.

There was perhaps no greater tribute to the old Roman talent for adapting to actual conditions than St. Benedict's regulation of diet. Food was rationed to each monk with meticulous care, but in times of great exertion or under conditions of exacting climate more than the usual portion was allowed. Wine was subject to similar regulation, not prohibited but limited to moderate use. And those of the northern races whose physical needs were greater than those of the milder south were granted larger portions still.

Christianity, the last creative force in the Roman World, had contributed a new scale of values and a new world for the future. But the Church empire did not last another thousand years through evangelical fervor alone. Out of the discredited elements of Roman civilization had arisen a new structure, and in the Christian Church that transcended the Roman state there was much that was still Roman.

The Conversion of the Barbarians

Henry Chadwick

In this informative essay, Henry Chadwick, a renowned historian, translator, and scholar of Christianity, surveys the missionary spread of Christian beliefs to the Germanic tribesmen, whom the Greeks and Romans had long referred to as the "barbarians." This process began in the fourth century and continued for some centuries after the collapse of the western Empire. Chadwick points out that at first most Roman leaders, including the popes and bishops, saw the barbarians as a temporary menace that would recede in time. Eventually, however, some more visionary leaders, such as Pope Gregory I, realized that the invaders had come to stay. Therefore, it was important that the church, if it wanted to survive and grow, convert those barbarians who had not already become Christians.

From the time of Constantine onwards the Roman emperors found that to obtain the best soldiers for the army they had to look to the Germanic tribesmen north of the long Rhine-Danube frontier, whose attacks had almost brought the empire to its knees during the middle years of the third century. Gradually the Goths became indispensable for the defence of the empire, and many of them reached high office; they began to take wives from Roman families. One of the emperor Julian's many complaints against Constantine was that he had promoted barbarians to important offices; but it was noticed by pagan observers that before long Julian himself was ap-

Excerpted from Henry Chadwick, *The Early Church* (Penguin, 1974). Copyright ©1967 by Henry Chadwick. Reprinted by permission of Penguin UK.

pointing a barbarian to the envied honour of the consulship. The appointments were resented by those who thought that the great Roman families should continue to hold a monopoly of such dignities. But at least the immigration was gradual and controlled. The situation changed quickly from 375 onwards. The pressure of the Huns from what is now south Russia precipitated an urgent move into the empire on the part of the Goths, and the movement became at once one of huge masses producing political and social disturbance. The Eastern half of the empire used barbarian generals almost as much as the West, but had a northern frontier that was relatively easy to control compared with the long indefensible Western frontier along the length of the Rhine and Danube. On 31 December 406 the Rhine froze, and the Vandals, Alans, and Suevi poured across into Gaul regardless of losses (the Vandals alone are said to have lost twenty thousand men at the river crossing). Two years later they were again on the move in search of food and pasture, and crossed the Pyrenees into Spain. In 429 the Vandals crossed the Straits of Gibraltar and swept into Africa, capturing Carthage in 439 where they established a pirate kingdom (a little larger than modern Tunisia) which lasted until Justinian's time.

The Germanic invasions produced chaos in the West. The collapse of Roman political control and administration was rapid, and the task of organizing local resistance often fell in the main to the bishops. One Hun attack on a town in Thrace was resisted only by the energy of the local bishop who placed a huge ballista under the patronage of St Thomas and then fired it himself to such purpose that he scored a direct hit on the barbarian chief. At Toulouse heroic tales were told of the leadership of the bishop during the siege. At first the barbarians were regarded as a merely temporary scourge that would be removed soon if people were truly penitent. To Salvian, the socialistic presbyter of Marseilles, they had been sent as a judgement on the vices of the empire in which the rich had wickedly oppressed the poor. But probably even Salvian did not suppose that the judgement was to be of long duration and that the invaders had come to stay.

Gothic Christianity

It was only slowly that the church took up the task of missionary work among the tribesmen; but, as the political threat grew, the hope of turning them into men of peace imparted high urgency to the project. With those who came into the empire during the fourth century some progress was made. In 381 the Council of Constantinople directed that 'the churches of God among the barbarian races must be governed according to custom', a reticent canon which at least informs us of the existence of groups of orthodox Germanic Christians within the empire. John Chrysostom preached in the Goths' church in Constantinople, where they used their own language for Bible and liturgy, and he also sent missionaries to the Goths in the Crimea and north of the Black Sea. . . .

Many of the Goths, however, were converted in the fourth century not to orthodoxy but to Arianism by Ulfila (*c.* 311–83). His mother's parents had been Cappadocian Christians carried off in a Gothic raid of the third century. In 341 he appeared in the empire as a member of a Gothic embassy to Constantius, was consecrated bishop by Eusebius of Constantinople, and returned to undertake a mission among the Visigoths for whom he invented the Gothic alphabet and translated the Bible. The Goths became the principal missionaries to the other Germanic tribes, each of which tended to become Christians a few years after settling within the empire. Such was the pattern of events with the Visigoths, Vandals, Suevi, Burgundians, Heruls, and Ostrogoths. Immigration into the civilized Roman world was felt to entail an acceptance of Christianity. One inscription from southern Gaul commemorates two barbarians in such a way as to imply that their racial origin was part of the stain washed away in baptism. But the fact that the barbarians' form of Christianity was mainly Arian was crucial. It meant that their attacks on the empire strongly reinforced the identification of the Catholics with the Roman imperial ideal. It also meant that as immigrants within the empire their racial distinctiveness was preserved by their religious dissent. The Franks alone among the invading German tribesmen were initially converted to Catholic orthodoxy with their king Clovis, 'the new Constantine', probably about 506; it was not until later in the sixth century that the Burgundians, Suevi, and Visigoths successively changed over from Arianism to Catholicism. For a period after the middle of the fifth century the Catholic communities in Gaul, Spain and especially North Africa suffered sporadic persecution from their Visigothic, Suevic, and Vandal rulers respectively. But most of the barbarians had a regard for Roman law and institutions, and for much of the time made it easy for Roman patriots to collaborate with them or at least not to feel impelled to interfere. Moreover, the Germanic tribes had a strong common interest with the empire in their efforts to resist the terrifying Huns under Attila (d. 453). The correspondence of Sidonius Apollinaris, a cultivated Gallic gentleman who became bishop of Clermont about 469, illustrates how the old Gallo-Roman aristocrats met the situation. They could either retire to their estates and libraries, or accept bishoprics and use the episcopal office as a vantage point for social and political cooperation with the barbarian government and at the same time as a guarantee of their own independence. The great bishops of southern Gaul in the sixth century, Caesarius of Arles and Avitus of Vienne, found it possible to work with their Visigothic and Burgundian rulers without compromising with Arianism in religion.

Italy Under Arian Gothic Rule

In Italy it was the same. The policy of collaboration with the barbarians kept at least a ghostly line of figurehead emperors in office until 476 (or 480), though power was now in the hands of barbarian army commanders. It ended in 476 because the barbarian general Odoacer decided to pension off the cipher emperor Romulus Augustulus at Ravenna and to make himself 'king' of Italy. Since the Renaissance the year 476 has come to be invested with deep symbolic importance as the moment of final collapse for the Western empire. At the time it was not seen in this light. Not much had changed. . . . At Constantinople there was still a powerful Roman emperor, claiming sovereignty over the West, and at his instigation Odoacer was attacked and killed by Theodoric the Ostrogoth. Theodoric in turn settled at Ravenna and took the title 'king', but at least he nominally acknowledged the ultimate sovereignty of the emperor at Constantinople, so long as his own independence of action was not restricted.

Under Theodoric's rule (493–526), the old Roman senatorial landowners, now committed to Christianity, continued to live much as they had in the past. Little changed. They valued their church, but treasured no less the glories of Rome and the poetry of Virgil. The Ostrogothic court did not discourage civilized pursuits. The high level of culture achieved by the Arian court at Ravenna may be seen today from the style of Theodoric's palace church (now S. Apollinare Nuovo) with its rich mosaics and noble decoration. . . .

But the ending of the church schism between Rome and Constantinople in 518–19 made Theodoric suspicious, with some reason, that the Byzantine emperor wanted to exploit the reunion for political purposes. The chief casualty of these suspicions was Boethius (c. 480–c. 524), an aristocratic scholar and rich senator. Boethius wrote not only about the doctrines of the Trinity and the Incarnation, but also works about Platonic and Aristotelian philosophy. . . . In 523 he fell under suspicion of treasonable dealings with Constantinople, and during his imprisonment before execution wrote his *Consolation of Philosophy*, remarkable for its strictly classical and pagan character almost untouched by any Christian motifs. Perhaps his Christianity did not go very deep.

Boethius probably regretted the existence of the Goths and thought about them as little as he could. It was different for his contemporary Cassiodorus (c. 485–582). Cassiodorus not only held high office with success under Theodoric and his successors, but also compiled a long history of the Goths. . . . He realized the pressing need, created by the new situation of the barbarian settlements, for educational institutions, and even planned an institute of higher studies at Rome modelled on the schools of Alexandria and Nisibis. But Justinian's decision to drive the Goths out of Italy ended all Cassiodorus' hopes of Romanizing and civilizing the barbarians in a common Christian and classical culture. He re-

tired to his picturesque estate at Squillace in Calabria to establish a monastic community called 'Vivarium' (fishpond),
designed to be a centre of religious studies. The foundation
was differentiated from others by the fact that Cassiodorus
tried to give his community a specially learned character.

Intellectual Versus Religious Ends

A few years earlier, about 529, Benedict of Nursia had
founded his monastery at Monte Cassino in central Italy.
The Benedictine monks were enjoined to spend on manual
labour such time as was not devoted to worship, divine reading, or meditation. No doubt some of this manual labour
was devoted to producing copies of the Bible, or Cassian, or

Early Missionary Methods

*Historian Justo Gonzalez explains how early Christian missionary
methods differed from those developed in later centuries.*

The enormous numerical growth of the church in its first centuries leads us to the question of what methods it used to achieve
such growth. The answer may surprise some modern Christians,
for the ancient church knew nothing of "evangelistic services" or
"revivals." On the contrary, in the early church worship centered
on communion, and only baptized Christians were admitted to
its celebration. Therefore, evangelism did not take place in
church services, but rather, as Celsus said, in kitchens, shops,
and markets. A few famous teachers, such as Justin and Origen,
held debates in their schools, and thus won some converts
among the intelligentsia. But the fact remains that most converts
were made by anonymous Christians whose witness led others to
their faith. The most dramatic form taken by such witness was
obviously that of suffering unto death, and it is for this reason
that the word "martyr," which originally meant "witness," took
on the meaning that it has for us. Finally, some Christians were
reputed for their miracles, which also won converts.

The most famous of these workers of miracles was Gregory
Thaumaturgus—a name that means "wonderworker." He was

Basil, which were recommended reading in the Benedictine Rule. In the time of Cassian early in the fifth century, manual labour, which might well take the form of writing a biblical manuscript, was prescribed as a remedy against idleness which made the monk peculiarly vulnerable to diabolical attack [i.e., assault by the devil].

In Cassiodorus' institution at Vivarium, however, this manual labour of copying manuscripts was to serve intellectual ends that were not narrowly religious. Vivarium was a lovely place with excellent fishing, conducive to pleasant recollection in tranquillity; and Cassiodorus' books were finely bound. He wanted his monks not merely to learn scripture by heart, as Benedict's might, but to understand it

---

from the region of Pontus, and had been converted through the learned witness of Origen. But upon returning to Pontus and becoming bishop of Neocaesarea, his great evangelistic success was due, not to his theological arguments, but to the miracles that he was said to perform. These were mostly miracles of healing, but we are also told that he could control the course of a river in flood, and that the apostles and the Virgin appeared to him and guided his work. Gregory was also one of the first to use a missionary method that has appeared again and again in later times: he substituted Christian festivals for the old pagan ones, and made sure that the Christian celebrations outdid the others.

Another surprising fact about the early expansion of Christianity is that, after the New Testament, very little is said of any missionaries going from place to place, like Paul and Barnabas had done. It is clear that the enormous spread of the Gospel in those first few centuries was not due to full-time missionaries, but rather to the many Christians who traveled for other reasons—slaves, merchants, exiles condemned to work in the mines, and the like.

Justo L. Gonzalez, *The Story of Christianity, vol. 1, The Early Church to the Dawn of the Reformation*. San Francisco: Harper and Row, 1984, pp. 98–99.

and expound it. Accordingly he laid down a course of secular studies according to a programme outlined by Augustine in his tract 'On Christian Doctrine'. . . .

In the Benedictine ideal the exclusive quest for God required detachment from all worldly studies and secular literature. The liberal humanism of Cassiodorus was eventually to be absorbed within the Benedictine tradition, in a confluence to which the Irish monks were to make some contribution, but it did not happen easily or quickly. When Pope Gregory the Great (540–604) renounced a distinguished secular career as prefect of Rome to become a monk, his model saint was Benedict of Nursia, whose biography he wrote in his *Dialogues* of 593. Gregory characteristically felt that conversion entailed turning his back on the world in all its forms, including literature. In the finely cut prose of his letters and sermons he seldom allowed himself a classical allusion, and his great achievements as pope (from 590) did not include the creation of a learned Roman clergy. Gregory's *Pastoral Rule* for clergy was other-worldly and monastic. It was only a late medieval legend which attributed to Gregory the destruction of the Palatine Library in Rome; but perhaps when he passed it he looked the other way. . . .

England, Ireland, and Scotland Converted

Italy in Gregory the Great's time was largely occupied by Lombard invaders, and the territory controlled by the Byzantine emperor's Exarch at Ravenna was relatively small. Rome, however, was a Byzantine city, and remained so through the seventh century. The pope was a subject of the emperor at Constantinople. But Gregory's personal prejudices were anti-Greek. He had also learnt from Augustine to think with a certain detachment about the connexion between the church and the empire. Above all, he recognized that the barbarian kingdoms of the West were not just transitory armies of occupation which would soon move on to other pastures, but a permanent social and political fact with which the church needed to come to terms. The Visigoths in Spain were now Catholic. In northern Gaul the Franks had been converted directly to Catholicism early in the sixth

century, and in the view of bishop Gregory of Tours
(*c.* 540–94), the historian of the Franks, their coming was a
divine deliverance sent to rescue a decadent imperial society
and to safeguard it from the corrupting Arianism of
Theodoric and the Ostrogoths. It seemed natural for Gregory the Great to adopt an equally positive attitude to the
Franks and Visigoths. Moreover, beyond them the pope
could see the need for a mission to the pagan Anglo-Saxons
in England.

Communications between Britain and the continent had
been temporarily endangered by the great sweep of the barbarian tribes into Gaul and Spain during 407–9. Britain
ceased to be a province within the empire and was left to
fend for itself against the invading Picts and Scots, for which
purpose the fateful decision was made to invoke the help of
some Saxons. But it was some considerable time before the
Saxon invaders swelled to such numbers that the British were
driven entirely into the western parts of the island. In the
first half of the fifth century at least, the British churches remained intact. . . . [A few decades later] Patrick was at work
as a missionary bishop in Ireland, founding monastic communities. In his autobiographical Confession, written in
awkward colloquial Latin, Patrick complained that in certain
quarters he was unkindly criticized for his mediocre educa-
tion; perhaps Ireland already possessed Christians with a superior Latin culture. At any rate by the sixth century the Irish
monasteries were becoming notable centres of study, including not only theology but also grammar and a lively interest
in the right methods of calculating the date of Easter, a matter in which the conservative and isolated Celts had come to
differ from the churches of the mainland. In 563 the Irish
monk Columba founded a monastery on Iona which extended the Christian mission to the wild tribes in Scotland.
His Pictish mission was not the first such undertaking, since
more than a century earlier Ninian seems to have established
a mission church at Whithorn (Candida Casa) in Galloway.
But the new monastery at Iona became an energetic centre
for the diffusion of Christianity and the Celtic monastic
ideals through Scotland and northern England.

In England and Wales the Saxon invaders gradually won the upper hand. The British Christians became divided by dissension, and about 540 a sombre picture of moral decline and administrative chaos was drawn by a deacon named Gildas. By the end of the sixth century the pagan kingdom of Kent, with its capital at Canterbury, dominated most of England south of the Humber. The Kentish king Ethelbert, however, married a Christian Frank. Pope Gregory saw in this the opportunity for a mission, and therefore sent the monk Augustine from Rome. On his way through Gaul Augustine appears to have been consecrated bishop, he landed at Thanet with a supporting body of monks, and proceeded to baptize Ethelbert and many of his people. It was a tribal conversion. Gregory's intention was that Augustine should establish the principal English bishoprics at the old Roman cities of London and York; but in practice the Kentish capital at Canterbury became and remained Augustine's see and chief missionary centre. Gradually, despite many obstacles and discouragements, the mission was extended to other parts of the country.

Gregory I, Creator of the Medieval Papacy

Howard F. Vos

A professor of history and archaeology at King's College in New York, Howard Vos is an authority on the history of Christianity. Here, he summarizes the importance of Pope Gregory I, called the Great, whom he credits with laying much of the organizational groundwork for the strong papacy that developed in the Middle Ages. Also, Vos shows, Gregory helped to refine church views on such fundamental practices as baptism, communion, and penance, and instigated missionary work that over time made Christianity the dominant faith of England. Last of the four great fathers of the early Church, Gregory can be seen as a transitional figure between ancient and medieval Christianity.

Gregory I, the Great (540–604), was one of the greatest leaders that the Roman church has ever had. Coming on the scene at the time of widespread political confusion with its consequent effects on the life and organization of the church, he became a stabilizing political influence and was largely responsible for the creation of the medieval papacy. Born into a noble, wealthy, and devout family, Gregory was for a while the prefect of Rome, the highest civil administrator in the city. This experience would later be invaluable to him. Gregory early turned to the monastic life as a way to glorify God, and he spent his inherited fortune to found seven monasteries. Pope Pelagius II called him back into public life, and from 579 to 586 he represented the Roman bishop at Constantinople. Elected bishop of Rome in 590, he strongly resisted the appointment but finally became reconciled to the calling. He much preferred the monastic life.

Civil Ruler of Italy

With the decline of imperial power in Italy, Gregory found himself raising an army to fight the Lombards [the northern European "barbarian" people who had descended into and taken control of much of Italy in the 560s], appointing commanders, conducting a war effort, caring for thousands of

---

Organizing the English Bishops

In this letter to his head missionary, Augustine (no relation to the great fifth-century writer of the same name), Gregory offers advice on how to organize the local English bishops and ensure that the English church will continue to grow.

To the most reverend and holy brother and fellow-bishop, Augustine, Gregory, servant of the servants of God. Although it is certain that the unspeakable rewards of the eternal kingdom are kept for those who labour for God Almighty, it is, however, necessary for us to render to them the benefits of honours, that from this recompense they may he able to labour more abundantly in the zeal of their spiritual work. And because the new Church of the English is brought to the grace of Almighty God by the bounty of the same Lord, and by your toil, we grant to you the use of the pall [a linen covering for the chalice used in holy communion] in the same to perform the solemnities of masses only, so that in several places you ordain twelve [several] bishops to be under your authority so far as that the bishop of the City of London ought always hereafter to be consecrated by his own synod and receive the pall of honour from this holy and Apostolic See which, by God's authority, I serve. Moreover we will that you send a bishop to York, whom you shall have seen fit to ordain—yet only so that if the same city shall receive the word of God along with the neighbouring places, he himself

refugees, and concluding a peace arrangement with the Lombards in 592–93. After the war was over, he did much to meet the needs of the poor in Rome and elsewhere. He became the real ruler of Rome and the virtual civil ruler of Italy in the last years of the sixth century. His administrative responsibility in Italy was important in the establishment of the Papal States [a region of central Italy largely ruled by the popes from the mid–eighth century to 1870]. Gregory's great achievement was to organize the papal government as an elaborate, smoothly functioning machine in a period when

also ordain twelve bishops, and enjoy the honour of metropolitan, because if our life last we intend, with the Lord's favour, to give him also the pall. But we will that he be subject to your authority, my brother, and that after your decease he should preside over the bishops he has ordained, but without being in any wise subject to the Bishop of London. Moreover, for the future, let there be this distinction of honour between the bishops of the City of London and of York, that he himself take the precedence who has been first ordained. But whatever things are for the zeal of Christ must he done by common counsel and harmonious action: let them arrange these concordantly, let them take right views and give effect to their views without any mutual misunderstanding. But you, my brother, shall have subject to you not only the bishops you ordain, and not solely those ordained by the Bishop of York, but as well all the priests of Britain, by the authority of our Lord Jesus Christ, so that from the lips and life of your holiness they may receive the form both of correct belief and of holy life, and fulfilling their office in faith and morals, may, when the Lord wills, attain the kingdom of heaven. May God keep you safe, most reverend brother. Dated the 22nd of June in the 19th year of the reign of Mauritius Tiberius, the most pious Augustus, in the 18th year after the consulship of the same lord, in the 4th indiction.

Henry Bettenson, ed., *Documents of the Christian Church*. London: Oxford University Press, 1967, pp. 152–53.

society in Italy and the West in general was falling irretrievably into decay. Significantly, he was spurred on in his work by the conviction that the end of the world was imminent.

Political Organization and Doctrinal Refinement

For many reasons Gregory was one of the most important popes in the history of Roman Catholicism. *First*, as noted above, *he transformed the bishopric of Rome into a papal system that endured through the Middle Ages.* His pontificate did much to establish the idea that the papacy was the supreme authority in the church. *Second, he introduced changes into the liturgy* [common rituals of worship] *and sought the standardization of it.* Although Gregory was not responsible for the type of chant that bears his name, he did much to promulgate its use in worship services and established schools for the training of singers.

Third, from a theological standpoint, his system served as something of a converging point for lines of thought found in the councils and in the Fathers. Though Gregory's theology was not original, he is important for his definition of dogma and his incorporation of elements of the popular piety of his day into the official teachings of the Roman Catholic church. He put tradition on an equal basis with scripture in determining dogma.

Though he accepted the Augustinian view of original sin, he held that through baptism sin was forgiven and faith implanted so that an individual might work the works of God. For sins committed subsequently penance was required. He expanded the concept of purgatory and converted the Eucharist from a sacrament into a sacrifice for redemption, having value for the living and the dead. He officially approved the invocation of saints and martyrs and the use of relics and amulets to reduce temporal punishments. His view of Christ and the Trinity followed the decisions of the ecumenical councils.

The First Monastic Pope

Fourth, he was important for his writings. The *Moralia*, a commentary on Job [a famous character from the Bible whom God rewarded for enduring an unusual amount of suffering], provided one of the patterns for the allegorical interpretation of Scripture common during the Middle Ages. His superstitious nature and that of the age is well displayed in his *Dialogues*, which concerns the lives and miracles of pious Fathers in Italy. And his *Pastoral Rule* was a practical work that instructed the bishop in the care of his flock and became the standard manual for the conduct of bishops. It was translated into Greek in his lifetime and into Anglo-Saxon by King Alfred the Great three hundred years later.

Gregory was a good preacher too, as evidenced by his forty sermons that have survived. They indicate a real concern for the spiritual and material needs of Christians in Rome. Gregory's writings have earned for him a place among the four great Latin doctors of the Western church: Ambrose, Augustine, Jerome, Gregory. *Fifth, Gregory promoted asceticism*, especially as he enforced the celibacy of the clergy and as he restored monastic discipline. The first pope to be monk, he was a great propagator of monasticism.

Last, Gregory possessed great missionary zeal. He sent forty monks to England in 596 under the leadership of Augustine (not the famous bishop of Hippo, who died in 430). Their success was pronounced, especially in the area of Canterbury, which became the religious capital of England and the seat of the archbishop.

Christianity in Later Ages

Tony Lane

The struggles and eventual triumph of the early Christian
Church, from the preaching of John the Baptist and Jesus
Christ through the rise of the papacy and conversion of
the barbarian tribes, had a profound impact on Europe
and much of the rest of world. In these formative years
Christianity was established as a major and highly influential religion. The legacy of the early Christian centuries
was that the beliefs that Paul, Tertullian, Ambrose, Augustine, Gregory, and so many others fought to defend
became the guiding force in the lives of untold millions of
individuals in hundreds of nation-states. In this excerpt
from his fascinating and useful recent book, *Exploring
Christian Thought*, scholar of religion Tony Lane gives a
brief but sweeping synopsis of the evolution of the faith
since Gregory's time. Lane traces the divisions, reforms,
competing beliefs, and major figures in the epic saga of
what is, if measured in the number of its adherents, the
world's most successful religion.

For Western Europe, the first part of the Middle Ages, until
about 1000, can aptly be called the Dark Ages. The western
half of the Roman Empire began to crumble before barbarian
invasions at the end of the fourth century, and in 410 the un-
thinkable happened—the city of Rome itself was taken. In
476 the last Western Emperor was deposed by a barbarian
Gothic king and the Western Empire had effectively ceased
to exist. The West continued to be subject to waves of inva-

sions—from Islam through Spain and from the Scandinavians in the north. This was a time of turmoil and anarchy, with the near collapse of civilization. The heritage of the past was in danger of being lost. . . . The church provided what little learning there was, especially through the monasteries, which were often oases of stability. There was a brief respite through the achievements of Charlemagne, who was crowned emperor in 800. He built a united and stable empire, in which civilization and learning were again possible. There was a brief flowering of scholarship during this 'Carolingian Renaissance'. . . . But before long Charlemagne's empire fragmented and Viking raids brought further setbacks.

Monastic and Scholastic Theology

Theology during this period was largely confined to the monasteries and is therefore called monastic theology. It was produced in an atmosphere of commitment and devotion, within the framework of a life lived according to the *Rule* of Benedict [ca. 480–543], for example. The goal was not the pursuit of knowledge for its own sake, but edification and worship. The approach was one of contemplation and adoration. The theologian was not a detached academic observer studying his material from outside, but a committed, involved participant.

On new year's eve, 1000, a crowd gathered at Rome, awaiting the end of the world. Midnight came, nothing happened and the pope, Sylvester II, blessed the crowd and sent them home. But Sylvester, formerly the scholar Gerbert of Aurillac, was himself one of the first-fruits of a new age. Greater stability was leading to the rebirth of Western civilization. The barbarian invaders had been 'converted' during the Dark Ages and by now all of Western Europe was nominally Christian— apart from the Jews in their ghettos and the Muslims in Spain.

The eleventh century was a time of new movements. There was a revival of monasticism, a new 'reform papacy' set about purging the church of corruption and there was a revival of learning. The theologian found himself faced with the question of the relation between faith (theology) and reason (philosophy). One modern writer says, 'The effort to harmonize reason and faith was the motive force of medieval Christian thought.' The impact of philosophy led to a new approach to theology: Scholastic theology or Scholasticism. Theology came to be studied outside of the cloister—in the university, and in other 'secular' (non-monastic) settings. The goal was objective intellectual knowledge. The approach was one of questioning, logic, speculation and disputation. It was more important for the theologian to be a trained philosopher than a godly man. Theology had become a detached objective science. This approach did not eliminate the older monastic approach, but it displaced it from the front line of theology.

The Impact of Philosophy

The impact of philosophy on theology began in the eleventh century with the emergence of reason (philosophy) as a method to be used in theology. Anselm used it to demonstrate the rationality of Christian doctrine. Reason had entered theology not (yet) as a means of defining Christian doctrine (which was based on revelation) but as a technique for defending and further understanding this faith. In the following century the role of reason was further expanded. Lawyers had begun to use philosophical methods to decide or arbitrate between conflicting authorities. . . .

In the thirteenth century, theology entered a new and more dangerous phase. Philosophy now appeared not just as a tool for use in theology but as a rival system of thought. This arose through the translation into Latin of Aristotle's metaphysical works. These writings presented a new way of looking at reality, a new worldview or philosophy of life as an alternative to Christianity. How was the challenge to be faced? For a time Aristotle's metaphysical writings were banned, but this was only a temporary measure to gain breathing space. Some tried to maintain the older Platonist worldview in opposition to the new Aristotelian outlook. The Franciscan theologian Bonaventure [1221–1274] led the field in doing this. But most influential in the long term was the approach of Thomas Aquinas [1225–1274], who attempted to make a synthesis between faith (theology) and reason (Aristotle). He set out to show that Aristotle's philosophy (rightly interpreted and corrected where necessary) could be consistently held alongside Christian theology.

Decline, Corruption, and Falling Numbers

The fourteenth and fifteenth centuries brought decline in the church, though some view them as the flowering of the Middle Ages. The papacy suffered its 'Babylonian Captivity', the popes being at Avignon and under French control from 1305 to 1377. The pope's return to Rome resulted almost immediately in the Great Schism (1378–1414), during which time there were always at least two rival popes. The religious orders also suffered decline. The fervour of the earlier centuries became rarer. Numbers fell and corruption increased.

In the fourteenth and fifteenth centuries there was also increasing scepticism about the possibility of harmonizing theology and philosophy. . . . Philosophy and theology went their separate ways, with theology retreating out of the 'natural' realm and relying increasingly on naked faith in God's revelation (the rationality of which could not be shown). . . .

The Middle Ages are often neglected, especially by Protestants. This is a mistake. The medieval period spans some thousand years—more than half the time from the birth of Jesus Christ to today. It may not be the most glorious period of church history, but it must be taken seriously as an important part of it. The medieval theologians wrestled with the problem of the relation between faith and reason. This remains a burning issue today and there is much to learn from the medieval experience. Then it was Aristotle, today it may be Darwin or Marx, but the basic issues remain the same.

The Way Paved for the Reformation

In 1500 papal supremacy over Christendom appeared secure. The Eastern churches, for long the centre of Christianity, had suffered a devastating blow in the capture of Constantinople by the Turks (1453). 'Conciliarism', the doctrine that the general council is the final authority in Christendom, over the pope, appeared to have been suppressed by repeated condemnations. But the foundations of papal power were not secure. Before long they were to be shaken by the earthquake of the Protestant Reformation, and some would prophesy that the pope would retain control over no more than Italy and Spain.

A number of factors paved the way for the Reformation. The late medieval papacy amply illustrated the maxim that absolute power corrupts absolutely, and there was considerable anti-papal feeling. . . . The church was in the vulnerable position of owning fabulous wealth while manifestly lacking the moral qualifications needed to justify her privileges to the populace. There was a revival of interest in the classical past, called 'Humanism' (not to be confused with today's atheist or agnostic Humanism). In Southern Europe this interest focussed mainly on the pagan Greek and Roman classics, but in the North there was a distinctively Christian Humanism, led by [Desiderius] Erasmus [ca. 1466–1536]. The keyword was 'back to the sources'—the Hebrew and Greek Bible and the early Christian Fathers. Humanists were bitingly critical of much contemporary church life—the lives of the popes and clergy, the state of the monasteries, the obscurities of medieval Scholastic theology. But when the Reformation came, Erasmus' disciples were divided. Some opted for reform at the cost of breaking with Rome, others reckoned unity to be of greater importance than reform.

The Reformers

The pioneer of the Reformation was Martin Luther [1483–1546]. He was prepared to stand alone against the might of the Roman Church. Before long his teaching had spread widely throughout Germany and then further afield to Eastern Europe and Scandinavia. But Lutheranism was not the only version of Protestantism. In Zurich, Ulrich Zwingli [1484–1531] began to preach reform at much the same time as Luther. While he was to some extent influenced by Luther, he was an independent thinker and differed from Luther on some matters. Before long Protestantism was split into two streams—Lutheran and Reformed (or Swiss) Protestantism. Zwingli died young and his place as the leading Reformed theologian was taken by the Frenchman John Calvin [1509–1564], with the result that the Reformed faith is often known as Calvinism.

Luther and Zwingli were *magisterial* Reformers—that is, they introduced reform in co-operation with the magistrates or rulers. They did not wish to break the link between the church and the state. Their aim was not to found a new church but to reform the old one. While there was reform of doctrine, the ideal of the state church, to which all citizens belonged, remained. But there were others for whom this was only half a reformation. The radical Reformers wanted to go further than the magisterial Reformers. This they did in a variety of ways. Some were 'rationalists' who questioned fundamental Christian doctrines like the Trinity. Some were 'spiritualists' who disparaged the Bible and all outward forms. They stressed the importance of the Holy Spirit speaking to the individual soul, the 'inner light'. Some were 'revolutionaries' who believed that the final struggle described in the Book of Revelation was about to take place and that the godly should establish the kingdom of God by force. But the 'evangelicals' were the largest and most important group. They desired a more thorough reform in the light of the Bible. They rejected the idea of a state church and infant baptism, which inevitably accompanied it. Their opponents seized on their practice of 'rebaptizing' those baptized in infancy and called them 'Anabaptists' or 'Rebaptizers'. This was a convenient label as rebaptism was already a capital offence. The Anabaptists were bitterly persecuted and largely exterminated, but their ideas survived and have become steadily more influential.

New Ideas, Including Deism

The Reformation found the Roman Catholic Church largely unprepared. But this situation did not continue for ever. The Council of Trent met in the middle of the century [in twenty-five sessions lasting from 1545 to 1563] to define Roman Catholic doctrine in an anti-Protestant direction and to introduce a programme of Catholic reform. The Jesuits, founded by Ignatius Loyola [1491–1556], were the shock troops of the Catholic Reformation and spearheaded the counter-attack on Protestantism. The heritage of medieval spirituality was not dead. . . .

The first fifty years of the Reformation was a period of new ideas. But the living creative movements of the early period were before long codified into detailed dogmatic systems. The three major confessions (Roman Catholicism, Lutheranism, Calvinism) all became increasingly preoccupied with a precise and intricate definition of their beliefs, and their energies were largely expended in controversy *within* the different confessions. These especially concerned questions of the relation between God's grace and human free-will. . . .

During most of the period from 1500 to 1800, theological debate took place mainly *within* these confessions. This was the period of confessional theology. But that has changed in the last two centuries.

During the medieval centuries and until about 1700, the truth of Christianity was largely unquestioned within Christendom. The medievals may have struggled with how to relate faith and reason. The Reformation debates concerned what is true Christianity. But whether Christianity is true was all but unquestioned. The eighteenth century saw the emergence of a significant movement, Deism, which advocated a simplified and 'pure' religion based on reason, as an alternative to the superstitions of Christian revelation. Deism was a *rival* religion, even if this may sometimes have been thinly disguised by the pretext of returning to primitive Christianity or to the essence of Christianity. Deism challenged the church from *outside* and by the end of the eighteenth century the theology of the churches remained predominantly orthodox. But during the nineteenth and twentieth centuries this picture has significantly altered.

Modern Challenges to the Faith

In the modern world, the Christian faith has had to face a wide range of challenges:

Rationalism. In the seventeenth century on a small scale and in the eighteenth century on a much larger scale, people began to attack Christianity in the name of reason. With Deism this took the form of a rival concept of God and religion; before long it was to become an attack on God and religion. In the nineteenth century atheism and agnosticism (a word coined by T.H. Huxley in 1870) became common for the first time in the Christian West. Confidence in the power of reason has waxed and waned in the modern world, but the attack on revelation has continued unabated. This has come at a time when all traditional authorities are being questioned—not just Christian authorities.

Science. Modern science emerged in the seventeenth century, in soil watered by Christianity. While the actual findings of science have had very little bearing on the truth or otherwise of Christianity, modern science has affected Christianity in other ways. The scientific method implies the testing of all claims and the refusal to accept any authority as beyond criticism. This method has been immensely successful in science and that has encouraged similar scepticism towards authority in other areas where it might not be so applicable. Also, modern science has given birth to technology, which has transformed our lives. It has helped to undermine man's sense of dependence upon God. As Bertrand Russell aptly put it, a fisherman in a sailing boat is more likely to pray than one in a motor boat. The benefits of technology also make it easier to live for this world alone and to forget about the next.

Historical Criticism. In the nineteenth century, historical criticism emerged. This was a new and more rigorous approach to history, practised by a new breed of professional historians. The critical historian thinks no longer in terms of *authorities*, which would rarely be questioned, but of *sources*, which must be questioned and tested. This approach has been applied to Christian history with devastating effect. The biblical records were analysed, often by people whose beliefs were far from orthodox. The Bible came to be seen less as an authority to be accepted and more as a source to be criticized. In the same way, the records of the life of Jesus Christ were examined and attempts were made to present a radically new picture of him. The history of Christian doctrine was also studied systematically and the ways in which it has changed over the ages came to light.

Secularization. As the Christian faith has ceased to command universal acceptance, society has turned to other ideological bases. For some time much of the world adopted a new secular 'religion', Marxism-Leninism [usually referred to as communism]. In the West, society is based on secular, non-religious assumptions. Religion is increasingly seen as a private affair for the individual, a matter for personal preference, like choosing to join a tennis club. This process has been encouraged by the emergence of a more pluralist society, where a variety of different religions are practised.

All of these changes have profoundly challenged Christian theology. Underlying them is the rejection of authority. Until the last century Christianity was all but universally seen in Christendom as a 'given', as a revelation from God which must be accepted by faith. Theological debates between and within different confessional traditions concerned the *identity* of that revelation. But since the last century the very idea of a revelation has been radically questioned—not just by unbelievers, but by theologians within the mainstream churches. It is true that the questioning of authority in the modern period has had some value in theology. There has been a healthy questioning of ill-founded assumptions. But the trouble is that while scepticism towards established authorities is the lifeblood of science, say, it is more like the kiss of death for theology. Any religion bearing more than a passing resemblance to Christianity must be based on some authority. If Christianity is about God revealing himself in Jesus Christ and rescuing man from his plight, there must be some submission before a given authoritative revelation. But to *what* must this submission be made (if at all) and on *what* terms? It is these questions which have divided Christian theologians in the modern era. The significant differences between theologians today lie less *between* different confessions and cut more *across* all confessions. This is becoming true even where the Protestant/Roman Catholic divide is concerned. Increasingly, groups of Protestants and Roman Catholics are finding that what unites them . . . is at least as significant as that which unites them to their fellow Protestants or Roman Catholics.

Appendix

Excerpts from Original Documents
Pertaining to the Rise of Christianity

Document 1: The Strict Life of the Qumran Community

The Dead Sea Scrolls reveal much about the everyday lives of the members of the Jewish Qumran community, who, prefiguring Christian monks in later centuries, sought to achieve religious purity by maintaining an austere monastic existence. The following excerpts from the long lists of community rules illustrate the extraordinarily strict discipline imposed on all members.

This is the rule for an Assembly of the congregation

Each man shall sit in his place: the Priests shall sit first, and the elders second, and all the rest of the people according to their rank. And thus shall they be questioned concerning the Law, and concerning any counsel or matter coming before the Congregation, each man bringing his knowledge to the Council of the Community.

No man shall interrupt a companion before his speech has ended, nor speak before a man of higher rank; each man shall speak in his turn. And in an Assembly of the Congregation no man shall speak without the consent of the Congregation, nor indeed of the Guardian of the Congregation. Should any man wish to speak to the Congregation, yet not be in a position to question the Council of the Community, let him rise to his feet and say: 'I have something to say to the Congregation.' If they command him to speak, he shall speak. . . .

These are the rules by which they shall judge at a Community (Court of) Inquiry

If one of them has lied deliberately in matters of property, he shall be excluded from the pure Meal of the Congregation for one year and shall do penance with respect to one quarter of his food.

Whoever has answered his companion with obstinacy, or has addressed him impatiently, going so far as to take no account of the dignity of his fellow by disobeying the order of a brother inscribed before him, he has taken the law into his own hand; therefore he shall do penance for one year [and shall be excluded].

Whoever has uttered the Name of the [Most] Venerable Being [shall be put to death]. But if he has blasphemed when frightened by affliction or for any other reason whatever, while reading the Book or praying, he shall be set apart and shall return to the Council of the Community no more.

If he has spoken in anger against one of the Priests inscribed in the Book, he shall do penance for one year and shall be excluded for his soul's sake from the pure Meal of the Congregation. But if he has spoken unwittingly, he shall do penance for six months.

Whoever has deliberately lied shall do penance for six months.

Whoever has deliberately insulted his companion unjustly shall do penance for one year and shall be excluded.

Whoever has deliberately deceived his companion by word or by deed shall do penance for six months. . . .

Whoever has lain down to sleep during an Assembly of the Congregation: thirty days. And likewise, whoever has left, without reason, an Assembly of the Congregation as many as three times during one Assembly, shall do penance for ten days. But if he has departed whilst they were standing he shall do penance for thirty days.

Whoever has gone naked before his companion, without having been obliged to do so, he shall do penance for six months.

Whoever has spat in an Assembly of the Congregation shall do penance for thirty days.

Whoever has been so poorly dressed that when drawing his hand from beneath his garment his nakedness has been seen, he shall do penance for thirty days. . . .

Whoever has murmured against the authority of the Community shall be expelled and shall not return. But if has murmured against his companion unjustly, he shall do penance for six months.

Should a man return whose spirit has so trembled before the authority of the Community that he has betrayed the truth and walked in the stubbornness of his heart, he shall do penance for two years. During the first year he shall not touch the pure Meal of the Congregation, and during the second year he shall not touch the Drink of the Congregation and shall sit below all the men of the Community. Then when his two years are completed, the Congregation shall consider his case, and if he is admitted he shall be inscribed in his rank and may then question concerning the Law.

C.K. Barrett, *The New Testament Background: Selected Documents*. San Francisco: Harper and Row, 1989, pp. 231–33.

Document 2: The Coming Battle Between Good and Evil

Like John the Baptist, Jesus, and a number of other Jewish preachers, the Qumran monks believed in the imminent arrival of God's kingdom, in which heavenly virtues would triumph over earthly evils. This apocalyptic vision is graphically illustrated in the colorful Qumran text describing the "war of the sons of light against the sons of darkness," excerpted here, which appears to address both the symbolic battle between good and evil and the real battle of God's chosen followers against the devil's human agents in the coming "last days."

This shall be a time of salvation for the people of God, an age of dominion for all the members of His company, and of everlasting destruction for all the company of Satan. The confusion of the sons of Japheth shall be [great] and Assyria shall fall unsuccoured. The dominion of the Kittim [non-Jewish enemies of the faithful, for instance, the Romans] shall come to an end and iniquity shall be vanquished, leaving no remnant; [for the sons] of darkness there shall be no escape. [The seasons of righteous]ness shall shine over all the ends of the earth; they shall go on shining until all the seasons of darkness are consumed and, at the season appointed by God, His exalted greatness shall shine eternally to the peace, blessing, glory, joy, and long life of all the sons of light.

On the day when the Kittim fall, there shall be battle and terrible carnage before the God of Israel, for that shall be the day appointed from ancient times for the battle of destruction of the sons of darkness. At that time, the assembly of gods and the hosts of men shall battle, causing great carnage; on the day of calamity, the sons of light shall battle with the company of darkness amid the shouts of a mighty multitude and the clamour of gods and men to (make manifest) the might of God. And it shall be a time of [great] tribulation for the people which God shall redeem; of all its afflictions none shall be as this, from its sudden beginning until its end in eternal redemption. . . .

Rise up, O Hero!
Lead off Thy captives, O Glorious One!
Gather up Thy spoils, O Author of Mighty deeds!
Lay Thine hand on the neck of Thine enemies
    and Thy feet on the pile of the slain!
Smite the nations, Thine adversaries,
    and devour the flesh of the sinner with Thy sword!
Fill thy land with glory
    and Thine inheritance with blessing!
Let there be a multitude of cattle in Thy fields,
    and in Thy palaces silver and gold and precious stones!

O Zion, rejoice greatly!

O Jerusalem, show thyself amidst jubilation!
Rejoice, all you cities of Judah;
keep your gates ever open
    that the hosts of the nations
    may be brought in!

Their kings shall serve you
    and all your oppressors shall bow down before you;
    [they shall lick] the dust [of your feet].
Shout for joy, [O daughters of] my people!
Deck yourselves with glorious jewels
    and rule over [the kingdoms of the nations!
Sovereignty shall be to the Lord]
    and everlasting dominion to Israel.

C.K. Barrett, *The New Testament Background: Selected Documents*. San Francisco: Harper and Row, 1989, pp. 247, 251.

Document 3: Josephus Describes the Essenes

Although the authors of the Dead Sea Scrolls did not specifically identify themselves as Essenes, most scholars believe the two groups were one and the same, largely based on comparisons between the Qumran writings and the following fascinating description of the Essenes given by the generally reliable first-century Jewish historian, Josephus. Many scholars also note the striking similarities, both physical and spiritual, between the Essenes as Josephus describes them and John the Baptist, who knew and influenced Jesus.

Among the Jews there are three schools of thought, whose adherents are called Pharisees, Sadducees, and Essenes respectively. The Essenes profess a severer discipline: they are Jews by birth and are peculiarly attached to each other. They eschew pleasure-seeking as a vice and regard temperance and mastery of the passions as virtue. Scorning wedlock, they select other men's children while still pliable and teachable, and fashion them after their own pattern—not that they wish to do away with marriage as a means of continuing the race, but they are afraid of the promiscuity of women and convinced that none of the sex remains faithful to one man. Contemptuous of wealth, they are communists to perfection, and none of them will be found to be better off than the rest: their rule is that novices admitted to the sect must surrender their property to the order, so that among them all neither humiliating poverty nor excessive wealth is ever seen, but each man's possessions go into the pool and as with brothers their entire property belongs to them all. Oil they regard as polluting, and if a man is unintentionally smeared with it he scrubs himself clean; for they think it desirable to keep the skin dry and always to wear white. Men to supervise the community's affairs are elected by show of hands, chosen for their tasks by universal suffrage.

They possess no one city but everywhere have large colonies. When adherents arrive from elsewhere, all local resources are put at their disposal as if they were their own, and men they have never seen before entertain them like old friends. And so when they travel they carry no baggage at all, but only weapons to keep off bandits. In every town one of the order is appointed specially to look after strangers and issue clothing and provisions. In dress and personal appearance they are like children in the care of a stern tutor. Neither garments nor shoes are changed till they are dropping to pieces or worn out with age. Among themselves nothing is bought or sold: everyone gives what he has to anybody in need and receives from him in return something he himself can use; and even without giving anything in return they are free to share the possessions of anyone they choose.

They show devotion to the Deity in a way all their own. Before the sun rises they do not utter a word on secular affairs, but offer to Him some traditional prayers as if beseeching Him to appear. After this their supervisors send every man to the craft he understands best, and they work assiduously till an hour before noon, when they again meet in one place and donning linen loincloths wash all over with cold water. After this purification they assemble in a building of their own which no one outside their community is allowed to enter; they then go into the refectory in a state of ritual cleanliness as if it was a holy temple and sit down in silence. Then the baker gives them their loaves in turn, and the cook sets before each man one plateful of one kind of food. The priest says grace before meat: to taste the food before this prayer is forbidden. After breakfast he offers a second prayer; for at beginning and end they give thanks to God as the Giver of life. Then removing their garments as sacred they go back to their work till evening. Returning once more they take supper in the same way, seating their guests beside them if any have arrived. Neither shouting nor disorder ever desecrates the house: in conversation each gives way to his neighbour in turn. To people outside the silence within seems like some dread mystery; it is the natural result of their unfailing sobriety and the restriction of their food and drink to a simple sufficiency.

In general they take no action without orders from the supervisors, but two things are left entirely to them—personal aid, and charity; they may of their own accord help any deserving person in need or supply the penniless with food. But gifts to their own kinsfolk require official sanction. Showing indignation only when justified, they keep their tempers under control; they champion good faith and serve the cause of peace. Every word they speak is more binding than an oath; swearing they reject as something worse than perjury, for they say a man is already condemned if he cannot be believed without God being named. . . .

Persons desirous of joining the sect are not immediately admitted. For a whole year a candidate is excluded but is required to observe the same rule of life as the members, receiving from them a hatchet, the loin-cloth mentioned above, and white garments. When he has given proof of his temperance during this period, he is associated more closely with the rule and permitted to share the purer waters of sanctification, though not yet admitted to the communal life. He has demonstrated his strength of purpose, but for two more years his character is tested, and if he is then seen to be worthy, he is accepted into the society. But before touching the communal food he must swear terrible oaths, first that he will revere the Godhead, and secondly that he will deal justly with men, will injure no one either of his own accord or at another's bidding, will always hate the wicked and co-operate with the good, and will keep faith at all times and with all men—especially with rulers, since all power is conferred by God. If he himself receives power, he will never abuse his authority and never by dress or additional ornament outshine those under him; he will always love truth and seek to convict liars, will keep his hands from stealing and his soul innocent of unholy gain, and will never hide anything from members of the sect or reveal any of their secrets to others, even if brought by violence to the point of death. . . .

Men convicted of major offences are expelled from the order, and the outcast often comes to a most miserable end, for bound as he is by oaths and customs, he cannot share the diet of nonmembers, so is forced to eat grass till his starved body wastes away and he dies. Charity compels them to take many offenders back when at their last gasp, since they feel that men tortured to the point of death have paid a sufficient penalty for their offences. In trying cases they are most careful and quite impartial, and the verdict is given by a jury of not less than a hundred: when they reach a decision there is no appeal. What they reverence most after God is the Lawgiver, and blasphemy against him is a capital offence. Obedience to older men and to the majority is a matter of principle: if ten sit down together one will not speak against the wish of the nine.

They are careful not to spit into the middle of other people or to the right, and they abstain from seventh-day work more rigidly than any other Jews; for not only do they prepare their meals the previous day so as to avoid lighting a fire on the Sabbath, but they do not venture to remove any utensil or to go and ease themselves. On other days they dig a hole a foot deep with their trenching-tool (for such is the hatchet they give to the novices) and draping their cloak round them so as not to affront the rays of the god, they squat over it; then they put the excavated soil back in the hole. On these occasions they choose the more secluded spots; and though emptying the bowels is quite natural, they are taught to wash after it, as if it defiled them. . . .

It is indeed their unshakable conviction that bodies are corruptible and the material composing them impermanent, whereas souls remain immortal for ever. Coming forth from the most rarefied ether they are trapped in the prison-house of the body as if drawn down by one of nature's spells; but once freed from the bonds of the flesh, as if released after years of slavery, they rejoice and soar aloft. Teaching the same doctrine as the sons of Greece, they declare that for the good souls there waits a home beyond the ocean, a place troubled by neither rain nor snow nor heat, but refreshed by the zephyr that blows ever gentle from the ocean. Bad souls they consign to a darksome, stormy abyss, full of punishments that know no end. . . . They tell these tales firstly because they believe souls to be immortal, and secondly in the hope of encouraging virtue and discouraging vice, since the good become better in their lifetime through the hope of a reward after death, and the propensities of the bad are restrained by the fear that, even if they are not caught in this life, after their dissolution they will undergo eternal punishment. This then is the religious teaching of the Essenes about the soul, providing an inescapable inducement to those who have once tasted their wisdom.

Josephus, *The Jewish War*, trans. G.A. Williamson. New York: Penguin Books, 1981, pp.133–37.

Document 4: John Baptizes Jesus

This excerpt from chapter three of the New Testament Gospel of Matthew, a core Christian document, first describes the appearance and spiritual work of the itinerant preacher John the Baptist, then goes on to tell how John encountered Jesus on the shore of the Jordan River.

3 In those days came John the Baptist, preaching in the wilderness of Judea, [2] "Repent, for the kingdom of heaven is at hand." [3] For this is he who was spoken of by the prophet Isaiah when he said,
"The voice of one crying in the wilderness:
Prepare the way of the Lord,
make his paths straight."
[4] Now John wore a garment of camel's hair, and a leather girdle around his waist; and his food was locusts and wild honey. [5] Then went out to him Jerusalem and all Judea and all the region about the Jordan, [6] and they were baptized by him in the river of Jordan, confessing their sins.

[7] But when he saw many of the Pharisees and Sad'ducees coming for baptism, he said to them, "You brood of vipers! Who warned you to flee from the wrath to come? [8] Bear fruit that befits repentance, [9] and do not presume to say to yourselves 'We have Abraham as our father'; for I tell you, God is able from these stones to raise up children to Abraham. [10] Even now the axe is laid to the root of the trees; every tree therefore that does not bear good fruit is cut down and thrown into the fire.

[11] "I baptize you with water for repentance, but he who is coming after me is mightier than I, whose sandals I am not worthy to carry; he will baptize you with the Holy Spirit and with fire. [12] His winnowing fork is in his hand, and he will clear his threshing floor and gather his wheat into the granary, but the chaff he will burn with unquenchable fire."

[13] Then Jesus came from Galilee to the Jordan to John, to be baptized by him. [14] John would have prevented him, saying, "I need to be baptized by you, and do you come to me?" [15] But Jesus answered him, "Let it be so now; for thus it is fitting for us to fulfil all righteousness." Then he consented. [16] And when Jesus was baptized, he went up immediately from the water, and behold, the heavens were opened and he saw the Spirit of God descending like a dove, and alighting on him; [17] and lo, a voice from heaven, saying, "This is my beloved Son, with whom I am well pleased."

Matthew 3.1–17, Holy Bible, Revised Standard Version. New York: Thomas Nelson and Sons, 1952.

Document 5: The Sermon on the Mount

Of the principal sayings and philosophical teachings attributed to Jesus, perhaps none is more basic and pivotal than his so-called Sermon on the Mount, which contains dozens of now immortal phrases.

23 And he went about all Galilee, teaching in their synagogues and

preaching the gospel of the kingdom and healing every disease and every infirmity among the people. [24] So his fame spread throughout all Syria, and they brought him all the sick, those afflicted with various diseases and pains, demoniacs, epileptics, and paralytics, and he healed them. [25] And great crowds followed him from Galilee and the Decap'olis and Jerusalem and Judea and from beyond the Jordan.

5 Seeing the crowds, he went up on the mountain, and when he sat down his disciples came to him. [2] And he opened his mouth and taught them, saying:

3 "Blessed are the poor in spirit, for theirs is the kingdom of heaven.

4 "Blessed are those who mourn, for they shall be comforted.

5 "Blessed are the meek, for they shall inherit the earth.

6 "Blessed are those who hunger and thirst for righteousness, for they shall be satisfied.

7 "Blessed are the merciful, for they shall obtain mercy.

8 "Blessed are the pure in heart, for they shall see God.

9 "Blessed are the peacemakers, for they shall be called sons of God.

10 "Blessed are those who are persecuted for righteousness' sake, for theirs is the kingdom of heaven.

11 "Blessed are you when men revile you and persecute you and utter all kinds of evil against you falsely on my account. [12] Rejoice and be glad, for your reward is great in heaven, for so men persecuted the prophets who were before you.

13 "You are the salt of the earth; but if salt has lost its taste, how shall its saltness be restored? It is no longer good for anything except to be thrown out and trodden under foot by men.

14 "You are the light of the world. A city set on a hill cannot be hid. [15] Nor do men light a lamp and put it under a bushel, but on a stand, and it gives light to all in the house. [16] Let your light so shine before men, that they may see your good works and give glory to your Father who is in heaven.

17 "Think not that I have come to abolish the law and the prophets; I have come not to abolish them but to fulfil them. [18] For truly, I say to you, till heaven and earth pass away, not an iota, not a dot, will pass from the law until all is accomplished. [19] Whoever then relaxes one of the least of these commandments and teaches men so, shall be called least in the kingdom of heaven; but he who does them and teaches them shall be called great in the kingdom of heaven. [20] For I tell you, unless your righteousness exceeds that of the scribes

and Pharisees, you will never enter the kingdom of heaven. . . .

38 "You have heard that it was said, 'An eye for an eye and a tooth for a tooth.' [39] But I say to you, Do not resist one who is evil. But if any one strikes you on the right cheek, turn to him the other also; [40] and if any one would sue you and take your coat, let him have your cloak as well; [41] and if any one forces you to go one mile, go with him two miles. [42] Give to him who begs from you, and do not refuse him who would borrow from you.

43 "You have heard that it was said, 'You shall love your neighbor and hate your enemy.' [44] But I say to you, Love your enemies and pray for those who persecute you, [45] so that you may be sons of your Father who is in heaven; for he makes his sun rise on the evil and on the good, and sends rain on the just and on the unjust. [46] For if you love those who love you, what reward have you? Do not even the tax collectors do the same? [47] And if you salute only your brethren, what more are you doing than others? Do not even the Gentiles do the same? [48] You, therefore, must be perfect, as your heavenly Father is perfect.

6 "Beware of practicing your piety before men in order to be seen by them; for then you will have no reward from your Father who is in heaven.

2 "Thus, when you give alms, sound no trumpet before you, as the hypocrites do in the synagogues and in the streets, that they may be praised by men. Truly, I say to you, they have their reward. [3] But when you give alms, do not let your left hand know what your right hand is doing, [4] so that your alms may be in secret; and your Father who sees in secret will reward you.

5 "And when you pray, you must not be like the hypocrites; for they love to stand and pray in the synagogues and at the street corners, that they may be seen by men. Truly, I say to you, they have their reward. [6] But when you pray, go into your room and shut the door and pray to your Father who is in secret; and your Father who sees in secret will reward you.

7 "And in praying do not heap up empty phrases as the Gentiles do; for they think that they will be heard for their many words. [8] Do not be like them, for your Father knows what you need before you ask him. [9] Pray then like this:

Our Father who art in heaven,
Hallowed be thy name.
[10] Thy kingdom come,
Thy will be done,
On earth as it is in heaven.

[11] Give us this day our daily bread;
[12] And forgive us our debts,
    As we also have forgiven our debtors;
[13] And lead us not into temptation,
    But deliver us from evil.

[14] For if you forgive men their trespasses, your heavenly Father also will forgive you; [15] but if you do not forgive men their trespasses, neither will your Father forgive your trespasses. . . .

22 "The eye is the lamp of the body. So, if your eye is sound, your whole body will be full of light; [23] but if your eye is not sound, your whole body will be full of darkness. If then the light in you is darkness, how great is the darkness!

24 "No one can serve two masters; for either he will hate the one and love the other, or he will be devoted to the one and despise the other. You cannot serve God and mammon.

25 "Therefore I tell you, do not be anxious about your life, what you shall eat or what you shall drink, nor about your body, what you shall put on. Is not life more than food, and the body more than clothing? [26] Look at the birds of the air; they neither sow nor reap nor gather into barns, and yet your heavenly Father feeds them. Are you not of more value than they? [27] And which of you by being anxious can add one cubit to his span of life? [28] And why are you anxious about clothing? Consider the lilies of the field, how they grow; they neither toil nor spin; [29] yet I tell you, even Solomon in all his glory was not arrayed like one of these. [30] But if God so clothes the grass of the field, which today is alive and tomorrow is thrown into the oven, will he not much more clothe you, O men of little faith? [31] Therefore do not be anxious, saying 'What shall we eat?' or 'What shall we drink?' or 'What shall we wear?' [32] For the Gentiles seek all these things; and your heavenly Father knows that you need them all. [33] But seek first his kingdom and his righteousness, and all these things shall be yours as well.

34 "Therefore do not be anxious about tomorrow, for tomorrow will be anxious for itself. Let the day's own trouble be sufficient for the day.

7 "Judge not, that you be not judged. [2] For with the judgment you pronounce you will be judged, and the measure you give will be the measure you get. [3] Why do you see the speck that is in your brother's eye, but do not notice the log that is in your own eye? [4] Or how can you say to your brother, 'Let me take the speck out of your eye,' when there is the log in your own eye? [5] You hypocrite, first take the log out of your own eye, and then you will see

clearly to take the speck out of your brother's eye.

6 "Do not give dogs what is holy; and do not throw your pearls before swine, lest they trample them underfoot and turn to attack you. . . .

15 "Beware of false prophets, who come to you in sheep's clothing but inwardly are ravenous wolves. [16] You will know them by their fruits. Are grapes gathered from thorns, or figs from thistles? [17] So, every sound tree bears good fruit, but the bad tree bears evil fruit. [18] A sound tree cannot bear evil fruit, nor can a bad tree bear good fruit. [19] Every tree that does not bear good fruit is cut down and thrown into the fire. [20] Thus you will know them by their fruits.

21 "Not every one who says to me, 'Lord, Lord,' shall enter the kingdom of heaven, but he who does the will of my Father who is in heaven. [22] On that day many will say to me, 'Lord, Lord, did we not prophesy in your name, and cast out demons in your name, and do many mighty works in your name?' [23] And then will I declare to them, 'I never knew you; depart from me, you evildoers.'

24 "Every one then who hears these words of mine and does them will be like a wise man who built his house upon the rock; [25] and the rain fell, and the floods came, and the winds blew and beat upon that house, but it did not fall, because it had been founded on the rock. [26] And every one who hears these words of mine and does not do them will be like a foolish man who built his house upon the sand; [27] and the rain fell, and the floods came, and the winds blew and beat against that house, and it fell; and great was the fall of it.

28 And when Jesus finished these sayings, the crowds were astonished at his teaching, [29] for he taught them as one who had authority, and not as their scribes.

Matthew 4.23–25, 5.1–48, 6.1–34, 7.1–29, Holy Bible, Revised Standard Version. New York: Thomas Nelson and Sons, 1952.

Document 6: The Judgment of Nations

Another of Jesus' core teachings greatly influenced the development of Christian belief and thought: His so-called Judgment of Nations, which describes how God will, in the final judgment, separate the blessed from the wicked, part of the sayings he supposedly delivered to his disciples shortly before the Last Supper.

31 "When the Son of man comes in his glory, and all the angels with him, then he will sit on his glorious throne. [32] Before him will be gathered all the nations, and he will separate them one from another as a shepherd separates the sheep from the goats, [33] and he

will place the sheep at his right hand, but the goats at the left. [34] Then the King will say to those at his right hand, 'Come, O blessed of my Father, inherit the kingdom prepared for you from the foundation of the world; [35] for I was hungry and you gave me food, I was thirsty and you gave me drink, I was a stranger and you welcomed me, [36] I was naked and you clothed me, I was sick and you visited me, I was in prison and you came to me.' [37] Then the righteous will answer him, 'Lord, when did we see thee hungry and feed thee, or thirsty and give thee drink? [38] And when did we see thee a stranger and welcome thee, or naked and clothe thee? [39] And when did we see thee sick or in prison and visit thee?' [40] And the King will answer them, 'Truly, I say to you, as you did it to one of the least of these my brethren, you did it to me.' [41] Then he will say to those at his left hand, 'Depart from me, you cursed, into the eternal fire prepared for the devil and his angels; [42] for I was hungry and you gave me no food, I was thirsty and you gave me no drink, [43] I was a stranger and you did not welcome me, naked and you did not clothe me, sick and in prison and you did not visit me.' [44] Then they also will answer, 'Lord, when did we see thee hungry or thirsty or a stranger or naked or sick or in prison, and did not minister to thee?' [45] Then he will answer them, 'Truly, I say to you, as you did it not to one of the least of these, you did it not to me.' [46] And they will go away into eternal punishment, but the righteous into eternal life."

Matthew 25.31–46, Holy Bible, Revised Standard Version. New York: Thomas Nelson and Sons, 1952.

Document 7: Paul on Love

After Jesus' death, when the early apostles began to spread the "good news" (from which the word gospel *is derived) about him, many of the concepts that became basic to Christianity crystallized in the lectures and writings of leading apostles. Most prominent among these was Paul, some of whose letters to Christian communities later became part of the New Testament. This excerpt from his first letter to the Corinthians is a moving and timeless expression of the power of love, which, along with faith and hope, abides and endures forever.*

13 If I speak in the tongues of men and of angels, but have not love, I am a noisy gong or a clanging cymbal. [2] And if I have prophetic powers, and understand all mysteries and all knowledge, and if I have all faith, so as to remove mountains, but have not love, I am nothing. [3] If I give away all I have, and if I deliver my body to be burned, but have not love, I gain nothing.

4 Love is patient and kind; love is not jealous or boastful; 5 it is not arrogant or rude. Love does not insist on its own way; it is not irritable or resentful; 6 it does not rejoice at wrong, but rejoices in the right. 7 Love bears all things, believes all things, hopes all things, endures all things.

8 Love never ends; as for prophecy, it will pass away; as for tongues, they will cease; as for knowledge, it will pass away. 9 For our knowledge is imperfect and our prophecy is imperfect; 10 but when the perfect comes, the imperfect will pass away. 11 When I was a child, I spoke like a child, I thought like a child, I reasoned like a child; when I became a man, I gave up childish ways. 12 For now we see in a mirror dimly, but then face to face. Now I know in part; then I shall understand fully, even as I have been fully understood. 13 So faith, hope, love abide, these three; but the greatest of these is love.

1 Corinthians 13.1–13, Holy Bible, Revised Standard Version. New York: Thomas Nelson and Sons, 1952.

Document 8: Paul on the Resurrection of Christ and Men

In their efforts to convert people to the new faith, Paul and other early Christian missionaries stressed Jesus' resurrection, which, as Paul states here, promised the ultimate resurrection and eternal life of all believers.

15 Now I would remind you, brethren, in what terms I preached to you the gospel, which you received, in which you stand, 2 by which you are saved, if you hold it fast—unless you believed in vain.

3 For I delivered to you as of first importance what I also received, that Christ died for our sins in accordance with the scriptures, 4 that he was buried, that he was raised on the third day in accordance with the scriptures, 5 and that he appeared to Cephas, then to the twelve. 6 Then he appeared to more than five hundred brethren at one time, most of whom are still alive, though some have fallen asleep. 7 Then he appeared to James, then to all the apostles. 8 Last of all, as to one untimely born, he appeared also to me. 9 For I am the least of the apostles, unfit to be called an apostle, because I persecuted the church of God. 10 But by the grace of God I am what I am, and his grace toward me was not in vain. On the contrary, I worked harder than any of them, though it was not I, but the grace of God which is with me. 11 Whether then it was I or they, so we preach and so you believed.

12 Now if Christ is preached as raised from the dead, how can some of you say that there is no resurrection of the dead? 13 But if there is no resurrection of the dead, then Christ has not been raised; 14 if Christ has not been raised, then our preaching is in vain

and your faith is in vain. [15] We are even found to be misrepresenting God, because we testified of God that he raised Christ, whom he did not raise if it is true that the dead are not raised. [16] For if the dead are not raised, then Christ has not been raised. [17] If Christ has not been raised, your faith is futile and you are still in your sins. [18] Then those also who have fallen asleep in Christ have perished. [19] If in this life we who are in Christ have only hope, we are of all men most to be pitied.

20 But in fact Christ has been raised from the dead, the first fruits of those who have fallen asleep. [21] For as by a man came death, by a man has come also the resurrection of the dead. [22] For as in Adam all die, so also in Christ shall all be made alive. [23] But each in his own order: Christ the first fruits, then at his coming those who belong to Christ. [24] Then comes the end, when he delivers the kingdom to God the Father after destroying every rule and every authority and power. [25] For he must reign until he has put all his enemies under his feet. [26] The last enemy to be destroyed is death. [27] "For God has put all things in subjection under his feet." But when it says, "All things are put in subjection under him," it is plain that he is excepted who put all things under him. [28] When all things are subjected to him, then the Son himself will also be subjected to him who put all things under him, that God may be everything to every one.

29 Otherwise, what do people mean by being baptized on behalf of the dead? If the dead are not raised at all, why are people baptized on their behalf? [30] Why am I in peril every hour? [31] I protest, brethren, by my pride in you which I have in Christ Jesus our Lord, I die every day! [32] What do I gain if, humanly speaking, I fought with beasts at Ephesus? If the dead are not raised, "Let us eat and drink, for tomorrow we die." [33] Do not be deceived: "Bad company ruins good morals." [34] Come to your right mind, and sin no more. For some have no knowledge of God. I say this to your shame.

35 But some one will ask, "How are the dead raised? With what kind of body do they come?" [36] You foolish man! What you sow does not come to life unless it dies. [37] And what you sow is not the body which is to be, but a bare kernel, perhaps of wheat or of some other grain. [38] But God gives it a body as he has chosen, and to each kind of seed its own body. [39] For not all flesh is alike, but there is one kind for men, another for animals, another for birds, and another for fish. [40] There are celestial bodies and there are terrestrial bodies; but the glory of the celestial is one, and the glory of the terrestrial is another. [41] There is one glory of the sun, and an-

other glory of the moon, and another glory of the stars; for star differs from star in glory.

42 So is it with the resurrection of the dead. What is sown is perishable, what is raised is imperishable. [43] It is sown in dishonor, it is raised in glory. It is sown in weakness, it is raised in power. [44] It is sown a physical body, it is raised a spiritual body. If there is a physical body, there is also a spiritual body. [45] Thus it is written, "The first man Adam became a living being"; the last Adam became a life-giving spirit. [46] But it is not the spiritual which is first but the physical, and then the spiritual. [47] The first man was from the earth, a man of dust; the second man is from heaven. [48] As was the man of dust, so are those who are of the dust; and as is the man of heaven, so are those who are of heaven. [49] Just as we have borne the image of the man of dust, we shall also bear the image of the man of heaven. [50] I tell you this, brethren: flesh and blood cannot inherit the kingdom of God, nor does the perishable inherit the imperishable.

51 Lo! I tell you a mystery. We shall not all sleep, but we shall all be changed, [52] in a moment, in the twinkling of an eye, at the last trumpet. For the trumpet will sound, and the dead will be raised imperishable, and we shall be changed. [53] For this perishable nature must put on the imperishable, and this mortal nature must put on immortality. [54] When the perishable puts on the imperishable, and the mortal puts on immortality, then shall come to pass the saying that is written:

"Death is swallowed up in victory." [55] "O death, where is thy victory?

O death, where is thy sting?"

1 Corinthians 13.1–13, Holy Bible, Revised Standard Version. New York: Thomas Nelson and Sons, 1952.

Document 9: Josephus Documents Jesus

The books of the New Testament are not the only ancient documents that mention Jesus. Helping to confirm the view that Jesus was a real historical figure is the following paragraph provided by Josephus in his Antiquities of the Jews, *written circa A.D. 93, about sixty years after Jesus' death. The bracketed phrases are those thought to have been added later by Christian scribes to make it seem as though Josephus advocated Jesus' divinity, which in fact the Jewish historian did not accept.*

About this time there lived Jesus, a wise man, [if indeed one ought to call him a man]. For he was one who wrought surprising feats and was a teacher of such people as accept the truth gladly. He won over many Jews and many of the Greeks. [He was the Messiah.]

When Pilate, upon hearing him accused by men of the highest standing amongst us, had condemned him to be crucified, those who had in the first place come to love him did not give up their affection for him. [On the third day he appeared to them restored to life, for the prophets of God had prophesied these and countless other marvellous things about him.] And the tribe of the Christians, so called after him, has still to this day not disappeared.

Josephus, *Antiquities of the Jews* 18.63, quoted in E.P. Sanders, *The Historical Figure of Jesus*. New York: Penguin Books, 1993, p. 298.

Document 10: Christianity Versus Greek Logic

During the first through third centuries, early Christian communities faced hatred, persecutions, and other obstacles. Some of the strongest opposition to Christian beliefs came from the Greeks, who felt that the unlimited and seemingly magical powers ascribed to the god of both the Jews and the Christians, were not logical or believable. The predominant Greek view (also held by most educated Romans) was that the gods dwelt within, not outside of, the cosmos and were therefore subject to, rather than able to circumvent, the limitations of certain immutable natural laws. The second-century Greek physician Galen ably expresses this view in this refutation of Christian "magic," which, failing to differentiate between Christians and Jews, criticizes the prophet Moses.

It is precisely this point [i.e., the idea that God could have made man out of a stone if he had wished to do so] in which our own opinion and that of Plato and of the other Greeks who follow the right method in the natural science differ from the position taken up by Moses. For the latter it seems enough to say that God simply willed the arrangement of matter and it was presently arranged in due order; for he believes everything to be possible with God, even should he wish to make a bull or a horse out of ashes. We, however, do not hold this; we say that certain things are impossible by nature and that God does not even attempt such things at all but that he chooses the best out of the possibilities of becoming. We say therefore that since *it was better* that the eyelashes should always be equal in length and number, it was not that he just willed and they were instantly there; for even if He should just will numberless times, they would never come into being in this manner out of a soft skin; and in particular, it was altogether impossible for them to stand erect unless fixed on something hard. We say thus that God is the cause both of the choice of the best in the products of creation themselves and of the selection of the matter. For since it was required, first that the eyelashes should stand erect and secondly that they should be kept equal in length and number, he planted them firmly in a cartilaginous body. If he had planted them in a soft and fleshy substance he would have suffered a worse failure not only than Moses but also than a bad general who plants a wall or a camp in marshy ground.

Galen, *On the Usefulness of the Parts of the Body* 11.14, quoted in Robert L. Wilken, *The Christians as the Romans Saw Them*. New Haven, CT: Yale University Press, 1984, pp. 86–87.

Document 11: The First Persecution

The first of many Roman persecutions of the Christians took place shortly after the terrible fire of A.D. 64, which destroyed large sections of the Empire's capital city. In this excerpt from his Annals, *one of the principal historical documents of the period, the great first-century Roman historian Tacitus captured the emperor Nero's merciless punishment of local Christians for their supposed role in starting the fire. This mention of Pontius Pilate's execution of Jesus is the only one to survive from a pagan Latin source.*

But neither human resources, nor imperial munificence, nor appeasement of the gods, eliminated sinister suspicions that the fire had been instigated. To suppress this rumour, Nero fabricated scapegoats—and punished with every refinement the notoriously depraved Christians (as they were popularly called). Their originator, Christ, had been executed in Tiberius' reign by the governor of Judaea, Pontius Pilatus. But in spite of this temporary setback the deadly superstition had broken out afresh, not only in Judaea (where the mischief had started) but even in Rome. All degraded and shameful practices collect and flourish in the capital.

First, Nero had self-acknowledged Christians arrested. Then, on their information, large numbers of others were condemned—not so much for incendiarism [arson] as for their anti-social tendencies. Their deaths were made farcical. Dressed in wild animals' skins, they were torn to pieces by dogs, or crucified, or made into torches to be ignited after dark as substitutes for daylight. Nero provided his Gardens for the spectacle, and exhibited displays in the Circus, at which he mingled with the crowd—or stood in a chariot, dressed as a charioteer. Despite their guilt as Christians, and the ruthless punishment it deserved, the victims were pitied. For it was felt that they were being sacrificed to one man's brutality rather shall to the national interest.

Tacitus, *Annals*, trans. Michael Grant. New York: Penguin Books, 1989, pp. 365–66.

Document 12: Early Christian Worship

This excerpt from one of the principal works of the early apologist Justin, penned about A.D. 150, explains the ritual of Holy Communion and also mentions the Gospels and the custom of collecting funds for charity. Note Justin's offhand recognition of the similarity between the Christian Eucharist and a rite practiced by the followers of Mithras.

After thus washing him who has been persuaded and has given his assent, we bring him to those that are called the brethren, where they are assembled, to offer prayers in common, both for ourselves and for him who has been illuminated and for all men everywhere, with all our hearts, that as we have learned the truth so we may also be counted worthy to be found good citizens and guardians of the commandments, that we may be saved with an eternal salvation.

We salute one another with a kiss when we have ended the prayers. Then is brought to the president of the brethren bread and a cup of water and wine. And he takes them and offers up praise and glory to the Father of all things, through the name of his Son and of the Holy Ghost, and gives thanks at length that we are deemed worthy of these things at his hand. When he has completed the prayers and thanksgiving all the people present assent by saying *Amen. Amen* in the Hebrew tongue signifies 'So be it.' When the president has given thanks and all the people have assented, those who are called deacons with us give to those present a portion of the Eucharistic bread and wine and water, and carry it away to those that are absent.

This food is called with us the Eucharist, and of it none is allowed to partake but he that believes that our teachings are true, and has been washed with the washing for the remission of sins and unto regeneration, and who so lives as Christ directed. For we do not receive them as ordinary food or ordinary drink; but as by the word of God, Jesus Christ our Saviour took flesh and blood for our salvation, so also, we are taught, the food blessed by the prayer of the word which we received from him, by which, through its transformation, our blood and flesh is nourished, this food is the flesh and blood of Jesus who was made flesh. For the Apostles in the memoirs made by them, which are called gospels, have thus narrated that the command was given; that Jesus took bread, gave thanks, and said, 'This do ye in remembrance of me; this is my body.' And he took the cup likewise and said, 'This is my blood,' and gave it to them alone. This very thing the evil demons imitated in the mysteries of Mithras, and commanded to be done. For, as you know, or can discover, bread and a cup of water are set out in the rites of initiation with the repetition of certain words.

Now we always thereafter remind one another of these things; and those that have the means assist them that are in need; and we visit one another continually. And at all our meals we bless the maker of all things through his son Jesus Christ and through the Holy Ghost. And on the day which is called the day of the sun there is an assembly of all who live in the towns or in the country; and the memoirs of the Apostles or the writings of the prophets are read, as long as time permits. Then the reader ceases, and the president speaks, admonishing us and exhorting us to imitate these excellent examples. Then we arise all together and offer prayers; and, as we said before, when we have concluded our prayer, bread is brought, and wine and water, and the president in like manner offers up prayers and thanksgivings with all his might; and the people assent with *Amen*; and there is the distribution and partaking by all of the Eucharistic elements; and to them that are not present they are sent by the hand of the deacons. And they that are prosperous and wish to do so give what they will, each after his choice. What is collected is deposited with the president, who gives aid to the orphans and widows and such as are in want by reason of sickness or other cause; and to those also that are in prison, and to strangers from abroad, in fact to all that are in need he is a protector.

We hold our common assembly on the day of the sun, because it is the first day, on which God put to flight darkness and chaos and made the world, and on the same day Jesus Christ our saviour rose from the dead; for on the day before that of Saturn they crucified him; and on the day after Saturn's day, the day of the sun, he appeared to his Apostles and disciples and taught them these things, which we have also handed on to you for your consideration.

Justin, *Apology* 65–67, quoted in Henry Bettenson, ed., *Documents of the Christian Church.* London: Oxford University Press, 1967, pp. 66–67.

Document 13: The Great Mother—Rival of Christ

One of the most vexing problems the early Christians encountered was competition from other eastern religions. Many eastern religions shared similar customs with Christianity, and most were much more popular and accepted. This description of the worship of perhaps the most popular of all, Cybele, the Great Mother, comes from The Nature of the Universe, *a magnificent poetic work by the first-century B.C. Roman thinker Lucretius.*

This is she who was hymned by Grecian poets adept in ancient lore. They pictured her a goddess, driving a chariot drawn by a yoke of lions. By this they signified that the whole mighty mass hangs in airy space: for earth cannot rest on earth. They harnessed wild beasts, because the fiercest of children cannot but be softened and subdued by the duty owed to parents. Upon her head they set a battlemented crown, because earth in select spots is fortified and bears the weight of cities. Decked with this emblem even now the image of the Holy Mother is borne about the world in solemn state. Various nations hail her with time-honoured ceremony as our Lady of Ida. To bear her company they appoint a Phrygian retinue, because they claim that crops were first created within the bounds of Phrygia [in Asia Minor] and spread thence throughout the earth. They give her eunuchs [castrated males] as attendant priests, to signify that those who have defied their mother's will and shown ingratitude to their father must be counted unworthy to bring forth living children into the sunlit world. A thunder of drums attends her, tight-stretched and pounded by palms, and a clash of hollow cymbals; hoarse-throated horns bray their deep warning, and the pierced flute thrills every heart with Phrygian strains. Weapons are carried before her, symbolic of rabid frenzy, to chasten the thankless and profane hearts of the rabble with dread of her divinity. So, when first she is escorted into some great city and mutely enriches mortals with wordless benediction, they strew her path all along the route with a lavish largesse of copper and silver and shadow the Mother and her retinue with a snow of roses. Next an armed band, whom the Greeks call Phrygian Curetes, joust together and join in rhythmic dances, merry with blood and nodding their heads to set their terrifying crests aflutter. They call to mind those . . . who once on a time in Crete, as the story goes, drowned the wailing of the infant Jove by dancing with swift feet, an armed band of boys around a boy, and rhythmically clashing bronze on bronze, lest Saturn should seize and crush him in his jaws and deal his mother's heart a wound that would not heal. That perhaps is why they attend in arms upon the Great Mother. Or else they signify that the goddess bids men be ready to defend their native earth staunchly by force of arms and resolve to shield their parents and do them credit. It may be claimed that all this is aptly and admirably devised. It is nevertheless far removed from the truth. For it is essential to the very nature of deity that it should enjoy immortal existence in utter tranquillity, aloof and detached from our affairs. It is free from all pain and peril, strong in its own resources, exempt from any need of us, indifferent to our merits and immune from anger.

Lucretius, *The Nature of the Universe* 2.600–680, trans. Ronald Latham. Baltimore: Penguin Books, 1962, pp. 77–79.

Document 14: A Foreign Goddess's Frenzied Worshipers

Both Christianity and Judaism rejected the use and worship of material idols. Indeed, one of the Ten Commandments handed down from God to Moses expressly forbids the making of "graven images." By contrast, the majority of pagan faiths freely used such images, as seen in this colorful description of a procession of worshipers of the goddess Atargatis, from the humorous novel The Golden Ass, *by the second-century Roman writer Apuleius.*

Next day the priests set out, clad in multicoloured garments and with features hideously made up; their faces were smeared with clay pigment, and their eyes were daubed with mascara. They had put on conical caps and saffron garments of linen and silk. Some wore white shirts decorated with purple stripes in spear-motifs pointing in different directions, and gathered up at the waist; they had yellow sandals on their feet. The goddess, who was attired in a garment of silk, they consigned to me to carry. Their arms were bared to the shoulder; they carried fearsome swords and axes; and they leapt about uttering ecstatic cries, for the pipe-music fired them to frenzied dancing.

After visiting several cottages in the course of their wanderings, they reached an estate belonging to a wealthy owner. As soon as they entered it they dashed forward frantically, making the place resound with their discordant wailing. For some time they bent their heads low and twisted their necks in supple movements, making their dangling locks rotate. Occasionally they would sink their teeth into their own flesh, and as a finale they each slashed their arms with the two-edged swords which they brandished. In the course of this performance, one of them behaved even more frenziedly. Drawing frequent breaths from deep within as though filled with the heaven-sent inspiration of a deity, he would pretend to be struck with madness—as if men visited by a divine presence are usually rendered feeble or sick, rather than raised to higher things!

But now observe how divine providence repaid him as he deserved. In loud, oracular tones he began lyingly to reproach and charge himself with having committed some wicked sin against the sacred tenets of his holy religion, and he proceeded to demand due punishment at his own hands for his sinful deed. He then seized the whip which these effeminates carry around as their distinctive possession. It is fringed with long, twisted tassels of wool, inset with several knuckle-bones from sheep. Wielding it, he scourged himself with lashes from this heavily knotted weapon, withstanding the pain of the blows in remarkable fashion by gritting his teeth. You could see the ground getting soaked with the filthy blood of the catamites as a result of the incisions of the swords and the blows of the whips. The sight made me considerably anxious, when I saw the blood gushing out in torrents from all these wounds, in case the stomach of the foreign goddess craved the taste of ass's blood, just as some people like to drink ass's milk.

Eventually exhaustion overtook them with this self-laceration, or at any rate they felt that they had had enough, so they called a halt to the torture. Many of those watching vied with each other in contributing coppers and even silver coins which the priests caught in the open folds of their garments. They also obtained a cask of wine, milk, cheeses, and a quantity of spelt and fine flour. Some people presented barley for the goddess's mount. All of this the priests raked in with greedy eagerness, stuffing it into sacks purposely brought for this windfall. They then heaped the sacks on my back, so that I doubled as a walking larder and a walking temple, for I was bowed down under the weight of the double burden.

Apuleius, *The Golden Ass* 8.27–28, trans. P.G. Walsh. New York: Oxford University Press, 1995, pp. 156–57.

Document 15: Why the Christians Do Not Act Like Romans

In this apology, perhaps the most often-quoted of all the early works in this genre, the second-century Christian writer Tertullian addresses his Roman critics and explains why the Christians do not worship the emperors or attend public games or the theater. He also argues that Christians are good businessmen who use their money to help society's less fortunate individuals.

"You do not," say you, "worship the gods; you do not offer sacrifice for the emperors." It follows by parity of reasoning that we do not sacrifice for others because we do not for ourselves—it follows from our not worshiping the gods. So we are accused of sacrilege and treason at once. That is the chief of the case against us—the whole of it, in fact. . . .

So now we have come to the second charge, the charge of treason against a majesty more august. For it is with greater fear and shrewder timidity that you watch Caesar than the Olympian Jove [Jupiter, chief god of the Romans] himself. . . . So that in this too you will be found irreligious to those gods of yours, when you show more fear for the rule of a man. In fact, among you perjury by all the gods together comes quicker than by the *genius* of a single Caesar. . . .

So that is why Christians are public enemies—because they will not give the emperors vain, false, and rash honors; because, being men of a true religion, they celebrate the emperors' festivals more in heart than in frolic. . . .

On the contrary, the name faction may properly be given to those who join to hate the good and honest, who shout for the blood of the innocent, who use as a pretext to defend their hatred the absurdity that they take the Christians to be the cause of every disaster to the state, of every misfortune of the people. If the Tiber reaches the walls, if the Nile does not rise to water the fields, if the sky does not move or the earth does, if there is famine, if there is plague, the cry at once arises: "The Christians to the lions!". . . .

For we invoke the eternal God, the true God, the living God for the safety of the emperors. . . . Looking up to heaven, the Christians—with hands outspread, because innocent, with head bare because we do not blush, yes! and without a prompter because we pray from the heart—are ever praying for all the emperors. We pray for a fortunate life for them, a secure rule, a safe house, brave armies, a faithful senate, a virtuous people, a peaceful world. . . .

Should not this sect have been classed among the legal associations, when it commits no such actions as are commonly feared from unlawful associations? For unless I am mistaken, the reason for prohibiting associations clearly lay in forethought for public order—to save the state from being torn into parties, a thing very likely to disturb election assemblies, public gatherings, local senates, meetings, even the public games, with the clashing and rivalry of partisans. . . . We, however, whom all the passion for glory and rank leave cold, have no need to combine; nothing is more foreign to us than the state. One state we recognize for all—the universe.

Your public games, too, we renounce, as heartily as we do their origins; we know these origins lie in superstition. . . . We have nothing to do, in speech, sight, or hearing, with the madness of the circus, the shamelessness of the theater, the savagery of the arena, the vanity of the gymnasium. Why should we offend you if we assume the existence of other pleasures? . . .

I will now show you the proceedings with which the Christian association occupies itself. I have proved they are not wrong; so now I will make you see they are good. We are a society with a common religious feeling, unity of discipline, a common bond of hope. We meet in gathering and congregation to approach God in prayer, massing our forces to surround Him. This violence that we do Him pleases God. We pray also for the emperors, for their ministers and those in authority, for the security of the world, for peace on earth, for postponement of the end. We meet to read the divine Scriptures. . . . Our presidents are elders of proved character, men who have reached this office not for a price but by character; for nothing that is God's goes for a price.

Even if there is a treasury of a sort, it is not made up of money paid in initiation fees, as if religion were a matter of contract. Every man once a month brings some modest contribution—or whenever he wishes, and only if he does wish, and if he can; for nobody is compelled; it is a voluntary offering. You might call them the trust funds of piety. For they are not spent upon banquets or drinking parties or thankless eating houses; but to feed the poor and to bury them, for boys and girls who lack property and parents, and then for slaves grown old and for shipwrecked mariners; and any who may be in mines, islands, or prisons, provided that it is for the sake of God's sect, become the pensioners of their confession. . . .

So we, who are united in mind and soul, have no hesitation about sharing property. All is common among us—except our wives. At that point we dissolve our partnership. . . .

Our dinner shows its idea in its name; it is called by the Greek name for love. . . . Since it turns on the duty of religion, it allows nothing vile, nothing immodest. We do not take our places at table until we have first partaken of prayer to God. Only so much is eaten as satisfies hunger, only so much drunk as meets the needs of the modest. . . . After water for the hands come the lights; and then each, from what he knows of the Holy Scriptures, or from his own heart, is called before the rest to sing to God. . . . Prayer in like manner ends the banquet. . . .

This gathering of Christians may properly be called illegal, if it is like illegal gatherings; may properly be condemned, if any complaint can be made against it such as are made against factions. To whose hurt have we ever met? We are when assembled just what we are when apart; taken together the same as singly; we injure none; we grieve none. When decent people, when good men gather, when the pious and when the chaste assemble, that is not to be called a faction. . . .

But there is another charge of wrong-doing made against us. We are said to be useless in business. How so, when we are human beings and live alongside of you—men with the same ways, the same dress and furniture, the same necessities of life? . . . So not without a *forum*, not without a meat market, not without baths, shops, workshops, stalls, and market days, and the other aspects of business, we live with you—in this world. We sail ships together with you, we serve in the army, go to the country, to market with you. Our skills and yours work together; our labor is openly at your service.

Tertullian, *Apology* 10.1; 28.2–3; 35.1; 40.1–2; 30.1, 4; 38–39; 42, quoted in Naphtali Lewis and Meyer Reinhold, eds., *Roman Civilization, Sourcebook 2: The Empire*. New York: Harper and Row, 1966, pp. 587–89.

Document 16: The Great Persecution

The most serious setback the early Christians encountered was the so-called great persecution, ordered by the emperors Diocletian and Galerius in 303. The Christian leader Eusebius, who eventually became adviser and biographer to the emperor Constantine, later penned this eyewitness account of some of the atrocities committed by Roman troops.

We saw with our very eyes the houses of prayer cast down to their foundations from top to bottom, and the inspired and sacred Scriptures committed to the flames in the midst of the market places, and the pastors of the churches, some shamefully hiding themselves here and there, others ignominiously captured and made a mockery by their enemies. . . .

It was the nineteenth year of the reign of Diocletian, and the month Dystrus, or March as the Romans would call it, in which, as the festival of the Savior's Passion was coming on, an imperial letter was everywhere promulgated, ordering the razing of the churches to the ground and the destruction of the Scriptures by fire, and proclaiming that those who held high positions would lose all civil rights, while those attached to households, if they persisted in their profession of Christianity, would be deprived of their liberty. Such was the first document against us. But not long afterwards we were further visited with other letters, and in them the order was given that the bishops of the churches should all, in every place, be first committed to prison, and then afterwards compelled by every kind of device to sacrifice. . . .

We shall mention the kind of death that one of them met, and leave our readers to gather from that instance what happened to the others. A certain man was publicly brought forward. . . . He was ordered to sacrifice; and, as he refused, the command was given that he should be raised on high naked and have his whole body torn with scourges [whippings] until he should give in and even against his will do what was bidden him. But when he remained unmoved even under these sufferings, they proceeded to mix vinegar and salt together and pour them into the mangled parts of his body, where the bones were already showing. And as he despised these pains also, a gridiron and fire were then produced, and the remnants of his body, just as if it were flesh for eating, were consumed by the fire, not all at once, in case he might find immediate release, but little by little; nor were those who placed him on the pyre allowed to desist until, after such sufferings, he should signify his assent to what was commanded. But he clung fixedly to his purpose, and triumphantly gave up the ghost in the midst of his tortures. . . .

Such were the things that were done in Nicomedia at the beginning of the persecution. But not long afterwards, when some in the district known as Melitene and again on the other hand when others in Syria had attempted to revolt against the government, an imperial command went forth that the bishops of the churches everywhere should be thrown into prison and bonds. And the spectacle of what followed surpasses all description; for in every place a countless number were shut up, and everywhere the prisons, that long ago had been prepared for murderers and grave robbers, were then filled with bishops and presbyters and deacons, readers and exorcists, so that there was no longer any room left for those condemned for wrongdoing.

Moreover, the first letter was followed by others, wherein the order had been given that those in prison should be allowed to go in liberty if they sacrificed, but if they refused should be mutilated by countless tortures. And then, once more, how could one here number the multitude of the martyrs in each province?

Eusebius, *Ecclesiastical History* 8.2,6, quoted in Naphtali Lewis and Meyer Reinhold, eds., *Roman Civilization, Sourcebook 2: The Empire*. New York: Harper and Row, 1966, pp. 599–600.

Document 17: The Conversion of Constantine

In this excerpt from Eusebius's biography of Constantine, the bishop tells the famous story of how that emperor came to adopt a Christian battle emblem, which supposedly ensured his great victory over Maxentius at the Milvian Bridge. This account was written at least twenty years after the fact. Moreover, Eusebius and his long-persecuted faith stood to gain much by his making a strong connection between Constantine and the Christian god. Therefore, modern historians are skeptical of some of the more fantastic details of the story.

Being convinced, however, that he [Constantine] needed some more powerful aid than his military forces could afford him, on account of the wicked and magical enchantments which were so diligently practiced by the tyrant [Maxentius], he sought Divine assistance, deeming the possession of arms and a numerous soldiery of secondary importance, but believing the cooperating power of

Deity invincible and not to be shaken. He considered, therefore, on what God he might rely for protection and assistance. While engaged in this enquiry, the thought occurred to him, that, of the many emperors who had preceded him, those who had rested their hopes in a multitude of gods, and served them with sacrifices and offerings, had in the first place been deceived by flattering predictions, and oracles which promised them all prosperity, and at last had met with an unhappy end, while not one of their gods had stood by to warn them of the impending wrath of heaven; while one alone who had pursued an entirely opposite course, who had condemned their error, and honored the Supreme God during his whole life, had found him to be the Saviour and Protector of his empire, and the Giver of every good thing. Reflecting on this . . . he judged it to be folly indeed to join in the idle worship of those who were no gods, and after such convincing evidence, to err from the truth; and therefore felt it incumbent on him to honor his father's God alone.

Accordingly he called on Him with earnest prayer and supplications that he would reveal to him who He was, and stretch forth His right hand to help him in his present difficulties. And while he was thus praying with fervent entreaty, a most marvelous sign appeared to him from heaven, the account of which it might have been hard to believe had it been related by any other person. But since the victorious emperor himself long afterwards declared it to the writer of this history, when he was honored with his acquaintance and society, and confirmed his statement by an oath, who could hesitate to accredit the relation, especially since the testimony of after-time has established its truth? He said that about noon, when the day was already beginning to decline, he saw with his own eyes the trophy of a cross of light in the heavens, above the sun, and bearing the inscription, CONQUER BY THIS. At this sight he himself was struck with amazement, and his whole army also, which followed him on this expedition, and witnessed the miracle.

He said, moreover, that he doubted within himself what the import of this apparition could be. And while he continued to ponder and reason on its meaning, night suddenly came on; then in his sleep the Christ of God appeared to him with the same sign which he had seen in the heavens, and commanded him to make a likeness of that sign which he had seen in the heavens, and to use it as a safeguard in all engagements with his enemies.

At the dawn of day he arose, and communicated the marvel to his friends: and then, calling together the workers in gold and precious stones, he sat in the midst of them, and described to them the figure of the sign he had seen, bidding them represent it in gold and precious stones. And this representation I myself have had an opportunity of seeing.

Now it was made in the following manner. A long spear, overlaid with gold, formed the figure of the cross by means of a transverse bar laid over it. On the top of the whole was fixed a wreath of gold and precious stones; and within this, the symbol of the Saviour's name, two letters indicating the name of Christ by means of its initial characters, the letter P being intersected by X in its centre [i.e., the Greek chi rho]: and these letters the emperor was in the habit of wearing on his helmet at a later period. From the cross-bar of the spear was suspended a cloth, a royal piece, covered with a profuse embroidery of most brilliant precious stones; and which, being also richly interlaced with gold, presented an indescribable degree of beauty to the beholder. This banner was of a square form, and the upright staff, whose lower section was of great length, bore a golden half-length portrait of the pious emperor and his children on its upper part, beneath the trophy of the cross, and immediately above the embroidered banner.

The emperor constantly made use of this sign of salvation as a safeguard against every adverse and hostile power, and commanded that others similar to it should be carried at the head of all his armies.

Eusebius, *Life of Constantine*, quoted in Brian Tierney, ed., *The Middle Ages, vol. 1, Sources of Medieval History*. New York: Knopf, 1973, pp. 15–16.

Document 18: The Christians Granted Religious Freedom at Last

In addition to chronicling the great persecution and the deeds of Constantine, Eusebius also performed an important boon to posterity by recording the major parts of the Edict of Milan. In the edict, made public in 313, Constantine and his eastern counterpart, Licinius, granted religious tolerance to the long-beleaguered Christians.

When under happy auspices I, Constantine Augustus, and I, Licinius Augustus, had come to Milan and held an inquiry about all matters such as pertain to the common advantage and good, these things along with the others that seemed to benefit the many, or rather, first and foremost, we resolved to issue decrees by which esteem and reverence for the Deity might be procured, that is, that we might give all Christians freedom of choice to follow the ritual which they wished, so that whatever is of the nature of the divine and heavenly might be propitious to us and to all those living under our authority. Accordingly, with sound and most correct reasoning we decided upon this our plan: that authority is to be refused no one at all to follow and to choose the observance or the form of worship of the Christians, and that authority be given to each one to devote his mind to that form of worship which he himself considers to be adapted to himself, in order that the Deity may be able in all things to provide for us His accustomed care and goodness. . . .

And since the same Christians had not only those places in which they used to assemble, but are known to have had others, also, which belonged not to individuals among them, but to the rightful claim of their whole body, that is, of the Christians, all these, in accordance with the law which we have just mentioned, you are to order to be restored without delay to the same Christians, that is, to their group and to each assembly, guarding clearly the aforementioned statement, that whoever restore the same places without compensation, even as we have already said, may hope for indemnification from our own generosity.

In all these matters you should exercise the utmost care for the aforementioned group of Christians, so that our order may be carried out as quickly as possible, and that also in this forethought may be exercised through our beneficence for the common and public peace. For by this means, as has been mentioned before, the divine zeal in our behalf, which we have already experienced in many things, will remain steadfast forever. And that the scope of this our decree and generosity may be brought to the knowledge of all, it is fitting that these matters as decreed by us be declared everywhere, and brought to the knowledge of all by being published at your order, so that the decree of this our generosity may escape the notice of no one.

Eusebius, *Ecclesiastical History*, 2 vols, trans. Roy J. Deferrari. Washington, DC: Catholic University of America Press, 1955, vol. 1, pp. 269–72.

Document 19: Arius Defends His Beliefs

This letter, dated circa 321 and addressed to Eusebius, bishop of Nicomedia (not his bishop/historian colleague of the same name), was written by Arius, the central figure in the Arian heresy that rocked the church and divided the faithful in the fourth century. Arius here clearly lays out both his own and his opponents' positions on the nature of Christ, who, the Arians believed, had a beginning, whereas God was timeless.

To his dearest lord, the man of God, the faithful and orthodox Eusebius, Arius, unjustly persecuted by Pope Alexander on account of that all-conquering truth which you also champion, sends greeting in the Lord.

Since my father Ammonius is going into Nicomedia, I thought it my duty to salute you by him, and at the same time to advise that naturally charitable disposition of yours, which you display towards the brethren for the sake of God and his Christ, how grievously the bishop attacks and persecutes us, and comes full tilt against us, so that he drives us from the city as atheists because we do not concur with him when he publicly preaches, 'God always, the Son always; at the same time the Father, at the same time the Son; the Son co-exists with God, unbegotten; he is ever-begotten, he is not born-by-begetting; neither by thought nor by any moment of time does God precede the Son; God always, Son always, the Son exists from God himself'.

Eusebius, your brother, Bishop of Caesarea, Theodotus, Paulinus, Athanasius, Gregory, Aetius, and all the other bishops of the East, have been condemned for saying that God existed, without beginning, before the Son; except Philogonius, Hellanicus and Macarius, men who are heretics and unlearned in the faith; some of whom say that the Son is an effluence, others a projection, others that he is co-unbegotten.

To these impieties we cannot even listen, even though the heretics threaten us with a thousand deaths. But what we say and think we both have taught and continue to teach; that the Son is not unbegotten, nor part of the unbegotten in any way, nor is he derived from any substance; but that by his own will and counsel he existed before times and ages fully God, only-begotten, unchangeable.

And before he was begotten or created or appointed or established, he did not exist; for he was not unbegotten. We are persecuted because we say that the Son has a beginning, but God is without beginning. For that reason we are persecuted, and because we say that he is from what is not. And this we say because he is neither part of God nor derived from any substance. For this we are persecuted; the rest you know.

I trust that you are strong in the Lord, mindful of our afflictions, a true fellow-disciple of Lucian, Eusebius.

Letter of Arius to Eusebius, Bishop of Nicomedia, quoted in Henry Bettenson, ed., *Documents of the Christian Church.* London: Oxford University Press, 1967, p. 39.

Document 20: The Council of Nicaea

The Council of Nicaea, convened by Constantine in 325, marked the first time that bishops from across the Mediterranean world met together in one place to decide on doctrine for all. This is the description given by the bishop/historian Eusebius of the meeting's setting and the emperor's memorable entrance.

Constantine summoned a general synod, inviting the bishops in all parts with honorary letters to be present as soon as possible. . . . At that time there were to be seen congregated in one place persons widely different from one another not only in spirit but also in physical appearance, and in the regions, places, and provinces from which they came. . . . From all the churches which had filled all Europe, Africa, and Asia, those who held the chief place among the servants of God assembled at the same time; and one sacred hall, extended as it were by the will of God, embraced in its compass Cilicians, Phoenicians, Arabs, Palestinians, Egyptians, Thebans, Libyans, and some coming from Mesopotamia. A bishop from Persia also participated in the synod, nor was Scythia absent from this body. Pontus, likewise Galatia, Pamphylia, and Cappadocia, Asia, too, and Phrygia provided their most carefully chosen persons. Thracians also, Macedonians, Achaeans, and Epirotes, and those who are situated at a very long distance beyond these were nonetheless present. . . . Present among the body were more than 250 bishops. . . .

But on the day fixed for the council which was to put an end to the controversies, when the various persons who composed the synod were at hand, in the very middle of the hall of the palace which seemed to surpass all the rest in size, there were many seats arranged in rows on both sides; and all who had been summoned entered and each sat down in his place. After the entire synod had seated itself with seeming modesty, all at first fell silent, awaiting the coming of the emperor. Soon one of those closest to the emperor, then a second and a third entered. Others, too, preceded—not, as customary, from among the soldiers and bodyguard, but only those of his advisers who professed the faith of Christ. And when the signal was given which announced the entry of the emperor, all rose, and finally he himself approached proceeding down the center . . . dazzling the eyes of all with the splendor of his purple robe and sparkling with fiery rays, as it were, adorned for the occasion as he was with an extraordinary splendor of gold and jewels. . . . As for his soul, it was sufficiently apparent that he was adorned with the fear of God and religion.

Eusebius, *Life of Constantine* 3.6–10, quoted in Naphtali Lewis and Meyer Reinhold, eds., *Roman Civilization, Sourcebook 2: The Empire.* New York: Harper and Row, 1966, pp. 609–10.

Document 21: The Arians Condemned

The most important decision made by the bishops gathered at Nicaea was to condemn as heresy the views of Arius and his followers, as expressed in this surviving official statement of the meeting. The controversy did not end here, however; many eastern bishops continued to support the Arian position, as did the later emperors Constantius II (337–361) and Valens (364–378). In addition, several barbarian converts to Christianity, including the Goths, adopted the Arian creed, ensuring its survival into the sixth century.

To the Church of the Alexandrians, holy, by the grace of God, and great, and to the beloved brethren throughout Egypt, Libya and Pentapolis, the bishops assembled at Nicaea, who constitute the great and holy Synod, send greeting in the Lord.

2. Since by the grace of God, and at the summons of our most God-beloved sovereign Constantine, a great and holy Synod has been constituted at Nicaea out of various cities and provinces, it appeared to us necessary, on all considerations, to send a letter to you from the sacred Synod, in order that you may be able to know what was discussed and examined, and what was decided and decreed.

3. In the first place, examination was made into the impiety and lawlessness of Arius and his followers, in the presence of our most God-beloved sovereign Constantine; and it was unanimously decided that his impious opinion should be anathematized, together with all the blasphemous sayings and expressions which he has uttered in his blasphemies, affirming that 'the Son of God is from what is not' and 'there was [a time] when he was not'; saying also that the Son of God, in virtue of his free-will, is capable of evil and good, and calling him a creature and a work. All these utterances the holy Synod anathematized, not enduring the hearing of so impious, or rather of so demented, an opinion, and such blasphemous sayings.

Letter of the Synod of Nicaea, 325, quoted in Henry Bettenson, ed., Documents of the Christian Church. London: Oxford University Press, 1967, pp. 40–41.

Document 22: The Christians Become the Persecutors

In the wake of Christianity's triumph as Rome's official religion, a remarkable reversal of fortunes that occurred over the course of the fourth century, Christians in their zeal turned on, condemned, and eventually even banned all non-Christian gods and rituals. Illustrative of increasing Christian intolerance for other faiths was the battle over the removal of the statue of Victory from the Roman Senate. Excerpts from the eloquent and impassioned arguments of the spokesmen for each side, the Roman aristo-crat Symmachus and the influential bishop Ambrose, are presented here.

Symmachus:

It is our task to watch on behalf of your Graces. The glory of these times makes it suitable that we defend the institutions of our ancestors and the rights and destiny of our country. That glory is all the greater when you understand that you may not do anything contrary to the custom of your ancestors. We demand then the restoration of that condition of religious affairs which was so long advantageous to the state. Let the rulers of each sect and of each opinion be counted up; a late one [the emperor Julian] practised the ceremonies of his ancestors, a later [the emperor Valentinian I] did not put them away. If the religion of old times does not make a precedent, let the connivance of the last [emperors] do so.

Who is so friendly with the barbarians as not to require an Altar of Victory? . . .

But even if the avoidance of such an omen were not sufficient, it would at least have been seemly to abstain from injuring us, we beseech you, as old men to leave to posterity what we received as boys. The love of custom is great. Justly did the act of the divine Constantius [who earlier removed the Statue of Victory] last but for a short time. All precedents ought to be avoided by you, which you know were soon abolished. We are anxious for the perma-nence of your glory and your name, that the time to come may find nothing which needs correction.

The divine Mind has distributed different guardians and differ-ent cults to different cities. As souls are separately given to infants as they are born, so to peoples the genius of their destiny. Here comes in the proof from advantage, which most of all vouches to man for the gods. For, since our reason is wholly clouded, whence does the knowledge of the gods more rightly come to us, than from the memory and evidence of prosperity? Now if a long pe-riod gives authority to religious customs, we ought to keep faith with so many centuries, and to follow our ancestors, as they hap-pily followed theirs.

Let us now suppose that Rome is present and addresses you in these words: "Excellent princes, fathers of your country, respect my years to which pious rites have brought me. Let me use the an-cestral ceremonies, for I do not repent of them. Let me live after my own fashion, for I am free. This worship subdued the world to my laws, these sacred rites repelled Hannibal from the walls. . . . Have I been reserved for this, that in my old age I should be blamed? I will consider what it is thought should be set in order, but tardy and discreditable is the reformation of old age."

We ask, then, for peace for the gods of our fathers and of our country. It is just that all worship should be considered as one. We look on the same stars, the sky is common, the same world surrounds us. What difference does it make by what pains each seeks the truth? We cannot attain to so great a secret by one road; but this discussion is rather for persons at ease, we offer now prayers, not conflict.

And let no one think that I am defending the cause of religion only, for from deeds of this kind have arisen all the misfortunes of the Roman race. The law of our ancestors honoured the Vestal Virgins and the ministers of the gods with a moderate maintenance and just privileges. This grant remained unassailed till the time of the degenerate money-changers, who turned the fund for the support of sacred chastity into hire for common porters. A general famine followed upon this, and a poor harvest disappointed the hopes of all the provinces. This was not the fault of the earth, we impute no evil influence to the stars. Mildew did not injure the crops, nor wild oats destroy the corn; the year failed through the sacrilege, for it was necessary that what was refused to religion should be denied to all.

Ambrose:

Ambrose, Bishop, to the most blessed prince and most gracious Emperor Valentianus, the august.

The illustrious Prefect of the city [Symmachus] has in his Memorial set forth three propositions which he considers of force: that Rome, as he says, asks for her rites again, that pay be given to her priests and Vestal Virgins, and that a general famine followed upon the refusal of the priests' stipends.

In his first proposition Rome complains with sad and tearful words, asking, as he says, for the restoration of the rites of her ancient ceremonies. These sacred rites, he says, repulsed Hannibal from the walls. . . . And so at the same time that the power of the sacred rites is proclaimed, their weakness is betrayed. So that Hannibal long insulted the Roman rites, and while the gods were fighting against him, arrived a conqueror at the very walls of the city. Why did they suffer themselves to be besieged, for whom their gods were fighting in arms? . . .

But why should I deny that their sacred rites fought for the Romans? For Hannibal also worshipped the same gods. Let them choose then which they will. If these sacred rites conquered in the Romans, then they were overcome in the Carthaginians; if they triumphed in the Carthaginians, they certainly did not benefit the Romans.

Let, then, that invidious complaint of the Roman people come to an end. Rome has given no such charge. She speaks with other words. "Why do you daily stain me with the useless blood of the harmless herd? Trophies of victory depend not on the entrails of the flocks, but on the strength of those who fight. I subdued the world by a different discipline. . . . Why do you bring forward the rites of our ancestors? I hate the rites of Neros. Why should I speak of the Emperors of two months, and the ends of rulers closely joined to their commencements? Or is it perchance a new thing for the barbarians to cross their boundaries? . . . I mourn over my downfall, my old age is tinged with that shameful bloodshed. I do not blush to be converted with the whole world in my old age. It is undoubtedly true that no age is too late to learn. Let that old age blush which cannot amend itself. Not the old age of years is worthy of praise but that of character. There is no shame in passing to better things. This alone was common to me with the barbarians, that of old I knew not God. Your sacrifice is a rite of being sprinkled with the blood of beasts. Why do you seek the voice of God in dead animals? Come and learn on earth the heavenly warfare; we live here, but our warfare is there. Let God Himself, Who made me, teach me the mystery of heaven, not man, who knew not himself. Whom rather than God should I believe concerning God? How can I believe you, who confess that you know not what you worship?"

By one road, says he, one cannot attain to so great a secret. What you know not, that we know by the voice of God. And what you seek by fancies, we have found out from the very Wisdom and Truth of God. Your ways, therefore, do not agree with ours. You implore peace for your gods from the Emperors, we ask for peace for the Emperors themselves from Christ. You worship the works of your own hands, we think it an offence that anything which can be made should be esteemed God. God wills not that He should be worshipped in stones. And, in fine, your philosophers themselves have ridiculed these things.

Symmachus, *On the Altar of Victory* and Ambrose, *Letter to Emperor Valentinian II*, quoted in Brian Tierney, ed., *The Middle Ages, vol. 1, Sources of Medieval History*. New York: Knopf, 1973, pp. 23–26.

Document 23: Augustine on Original Sin

The most important of the late Latin Christian writers, especially to later ages, Augustine (354–430) helped to crystallize and institutionalize many existing or developing aspects of church doctrine, including that of original sin, the notion that human beings are born as sinners because of Adam's transgressions against God in the Garden of Eden. This statement about Adam's "corrupt and condemned children" comes from Augustine's long and highly influential masterwork, The City of God.

For God, the author of natures, not of vices, created man upright; but man, being of his own will corrupted and justly condemned, begot corrupted and condemned children. For we all were in that one man, since we all were that one man, who fell into sin by the woman who was made from him before the sin. For not yet was the particular form created and distributed to us, in which we as individuals were to live, but already the seminal nature was there from which we were to be propagated; and this being vitiated by sin, and bound by the chain of death, and justly condemned, man could not be born of man in any other state. And thus, from the bad use of free will, there originated the whole train of evil, which, with its concatenation of miseries, convoys the human race from its depraved origin, as from a corrupt root, on to the destruction of the second death, which has no end, those only being excepted who are freed by the grace of God. . . .

It may perhaps be supposed that because God said, "Ye shall die the death," and not "deaths," we should understand only that death which occurs when the soul is deserted by God, Who is its life; for it was not deserted by God, and so deserted Him, but deserted Him, and so was deserted by Him. For its own will was the originator of its evil, as God was the originator of its motions towards good, both in making it when it was not and in remaking it when it had fallen and perished. But though we suppose that God meant only this death, and that the words, "In the day ye eat of it ye shall die the death," should be understood as meaning, "In the day ye desert me in disobedience, I will desert you in justice," yet assuredly in this death the other deaths also were threatened, which were its inevitable consequence. For in the first stirring of the disobedient motion which was felt in the flesh of the disobedient soul, and which caused our first parents to cover their shame, one death indeed is experienced, that, namely, which occurs when God forsakes the soul. (This was intimated by the words He uttered, when the man, stupefied by fear, had hid himself, "Adam, where art thou?"— words which He used not in ignorance or inquiry, but warning him to consider where he was, since God was not with him.) But when the soul itself forsook the body, corrupted and decayed with age, the other death was experienced of which God had spoken in pronouncing man's sentence, "Earth thou art, and unto earth shalt thou return." And of these two deaths that first death of the whole man is composed. And this first death is finally followed by the second, unless man be freed by grace. For the body would not return to the earth from which it was made, save only by the death proper to itself, which occurs when it is forsaken of the soul, its life. And therefore it is agreed among all Christians who truthfully hold the Catholic faith that we are subject to the death of the body, not by the law of nature, by which God ordained no death for man, but by His righteous infliction on account of sin; for God, taking vengeance on sin, said to the man, in whom we all then were, "Dust thou art, and unto dust shalt thou return."

Augustine, *The City of God* 13.14–15, trans. Marcus Dods, in Mortimer Adler, ed., *Great Books of the Western World*, vol. 18. Chicago: Encyclopaedia Britannica, 1952, p. 366.

Document 24: Leo's Vision of Jesus' Nature

In his famous Tome, *composed in 449 and excerpted here, Leo explained what he and many other church leaders saw as Jesus' unique nature, essentially one being with two manifestations, one of them human, the other divine. This helped to establish the traditional right of the Roman holy see to determine official spiritual doctrines for the entire Christian community.*

God is believed to be both Almighty and Father; it follows that the Son is shown to be co-eternal with him, differing in no respect from the Father. For he was born God of God, Almighty of Almighty, co-eternal of eternal; not later in time, not inferior in power, not dissimilar in glory, not divided in essence. The same only-begotten, eternal Son of the eternal Father was born of the Holy Ghost and the Virgin Mary. But this birth in time has taken nothing from, and added nothing to, that divine eternal nativity, but has bestowed itself wholly on the restoration of man, who had been deceived: that it might overcome death and by its own virtue overthrow the devil who had the power of death. For we could not overcome the author of sin and death, unless he had taken our nature and made it his own, whom sin could not defile nor death retain, since he was conceived of the Holy Spirit, in the womb of his Virgin Mother, whose virginity remained entire in his birth as in his conception. . . . That birth, uniquely marvellous and marvellously unique, ought not to be understood in such a way as to preclude the distinctive properties of the kind [i.e. of humanity] through the new mode of creation. For it is true that the Holy Spirit gave fruitfulness to the Virgin, but the reality of his body was received from her body. . . .

III. Thus the properties of each nature and substance were preserved entire, and came together to form one person. Humility was assumed by majesty, weakness by strength, mortality by eternity; and to pay the debt that we had incurred, an inviolable nature was united to a nature that can suffer. And so, to fulfil the conditions of our healing, the man Jesus Christ, one and the same mediator between God and man, was able to die in respect of the one, unable to die in respect of the other.

Thus there was born true God in the entire and perfect nature of true man, complete in his own properties, complete in ours. By 'ours' I mean those which the Creator formed in us at the beginning, which he assumed in order to restore; for in the Saviour there was no trace of the properties which the deceiver brought in, and which man, being deceived, allowed to enter. He did not become partaker of our sins because he entered into fellowship with human infirmities. He assumed the form of a servant without the stain of sin, making the human properties greater, but not detracting from the divine. For that 'emptying of himself,' whereby the invisible rendered himself visible, and the Creator and Lord of all willed to be a mortal, was a condescension of compassion, not a failure of power. Accordingly, he who made man, while he remained in the form of God, was himself made man in the form of a servant. Each nature preserves its own characteristics without diminution, so that the form of a servant does not detract from the form of God.

Henry Bettenson, ed., *Documents of the Christian Church*. London: Oxford University Press, 1967, pp. 49–50.

Document 25: Pope Gregory I Converts the English

The final major aspect of early Christianity's triumph was the conversion of those of Europe's barbarian tribes that had not yet accepted Christ. One of the most important figures in this ongoing effort was Pope Gregory I, called the Great (540–604). In 596 or 597, he sent a group of about forty young monks, led by a Roman monastic prior named Augustine (no relation to the author of The City of God) *to England; there, Augustine founded a cathedral and a combination school and seminary at Canterbury, which subsequently became the center of the Church of England. Gregory wrote the following letter, describing this missionary work, to a colleague in about 598.*

Gregory to Eulogius, bishop of Alexandria. . . . Since your good deeds bear fruit in which you rejoice as well as others, I am making you a return for benefits received by sending news of the same kind. And this is that whilst the people of the English, placed in a corner of the world, still remained without faith, worshipping stocks and stones, I resolved, aided in this by your prayers, that I ought with God's assistance to send to this people a monk [Augustine] from my monastery to preach. He, by licence given from me, was made bishop by the bishops of the Germanies and with their encouragement was brought on his way to the people aforesaid in the ends of the world; and already letters have reached us telling of his safety and of his work, that both he and they who were sent with him are radiant with such great miracles amongst this people, that they seem to reproduce the powers of the apostles in the signs that they display. Indeed, on the solemn feast of the Lord's Nativity now past, more than ten thousand Angles, according to our information, were baptized by the same our brother and fellow-bishop. I have told you this that you may know not only what you do among the people of Alexandria by speaking, but also what you accomplish in the ends of the world by prayer. For your prayers are in that place where you are not, whilst your holy deeds are exhibited in that place where you are.

Pope Gregory I, *Letter to Eulogius, Patriarch of Alexandria*, quoted in Henry Bettenson, ed., *Documents of the Christian Church*. London: Oxford University Press, 1967, pp. 151–52.

Chronology

B.C.

ca. 250–A.D. 68
Approximate dates of the writing of the Dead Sea Scrolls, widely believed to be the work of the Essenes, a monastic Jewish sect whose beliefs may have influenced Jesus.

27
Octavian, winner of the last of several civil wars to rock the Roman Republic, is hailed as Augustus Caesar, marking the emergence of the autocratic Roman Empire, which will dominate the Mediterranean world for the next five centuries.

ca.4
Approximate date of Jesus' birth (a modern correction of an error made by the Christian monk Dionysius Exiguus while devising the B.C.–A.D. dating system in the sixth century).

A.D.

6
Judaea, the section of Palestine roughly corresponding to the ancient Jewish kingdom of Judah, becomes a Roman province.

26
Pontius Pilate, who will later condemn Jesus to death, becomes prefect of Judaea.

ca. 30
Jesus is tried for and convicted of sedition and crucified in Jerusalem.

ca. 36–67
The ministry of the apostle Paul, who saw the wisdom of converting gentiles as well as Jews to the belief that Jesus was the son of God.

64
After a fire devastates much of the city of Rome, the emperor Nero accuses the Christians of starting the blaze and launches the first of many anti-Christian persecutions.

70

At the climax of a bloody Jewish rebellion against Roman rule, the Romans sack Jerusalem, decimating the ranks of Jewish Christians, who will thereafter steadily disappear.

ca. 70–100

The four major Gospels later accepted into the New Testament are written, but at this time remain anonymous.

ca. 140

Christian leaders begin to write apologies, statements explaining and defending Christian beliefs.

ca. 140–200

The books making up the official canon of the New Testament are slowly debated and accepted, including the four Gospels, which finally receive names (Matthew, Mark, Luke, and John).

ca. 160

Birth of Tertullian, who writes the first apology in Latin (rather than Greek).

ca. 184

Birth of the highly influential apologist Origen.

249–251

The Christians are severely persecuted on orders of the Roman emperor Decius.

ca. 270s

The Christian monastic movement (in which people show their devotion to God by becoming hermits or monks) begins.

303–311

The Christians suffer their most widespread and brutal persecution ever, largely instigated by the eastern emperor Galerius.

312

The emperor Constantine I wins a stunning victory over his chief rival at Rome's Milvian Bridge, giving him complete authority in the West.

313

In concert with the eastern emperor Licinius, Constantine announces the so-called Edict of Milan, granting the Christians complete tolerance.

316
Urged on by a majority of Christian leaders, Constantine denounces the Donatists, Christians who argue that priests and others who surrendered the Scriptures during the last great persecution are impure.

ca. 320
The first version of St. Peter's Basilica is erected in Rome.

325
Bishops from throughout the Mediterranean world meet for the first time at Nicaea, in Asia Minor, and take an official stand against the Arians, Christians who believe that Jesus was posterior, or inferior, to God.

330
Constantine founds Constantinople (the "city of Constantine"), the first Christian city, on the Bosporus strait.

337
Constantine is baptized a Christian and dies.

339
Death of Eusebius, Constantine's biographer and the first scholar to write a history of the Church.

354–430
Life of the pivotal Christian theologian Augustine, whose *Confessions* and *City of God* will later exert a profound influence over medieval and early modern Christian thought.

361–363
Reign of Julian, the last pagan emperor, who unsuccessfully attempts to halt the growth of Christian political and spiritual authority in the Roman Empire.

392
The emperor Theodosius issues an imperial decree banning non-Christian worship; nevertheless, most pagans continue to observe their beliefs in private.

ca. 397
Death of the dynamic bishop Ambrose, whose influence over several emperors was crucial in Christianity's triumph as Rome's official religion.

420
Death of Jerome, the prominent Christian thinker and writer whose translation of the Bible becomes the standard for centuries to come.

476
After more than a century of political, economic, and military decline, the western Roman Empire falls into the hands of "barbarian" rulers. Some of these Germanic tribes, including the Goths, have already been Christianized; others will become so in succeeding centuries.

540–604
Life of Gregory I, whose organizational work helps lay the groundwork for the success of the medieval papacy.

596
Gregory sends a mission to England to train bishops and convert local barbarian pagans; this effort eventually leads to the growth of the Church of England, one of the great bastions of European Christianity.

For Further Research

Collections of Original Documents Pertaining to the Rise of Christianity

Augustine, *The City of God*. Trans. Henry Bettenson. New York: Penguin, 1984; and *Major Works*, in Mortimer Adler, ed., *Great Books of the Western World*, vol. 18. Chicago: Encyclopaedia Britannica, 1952.

Apuleius, *The Golden Ass*. Trans. P.G. Walsh. New York: Oxford University Press, 1995.

Nels M. Bailkey, ed., *Readings in Ancient History: From Gilgamesh to Diocletian*. Lexington, MA: D.C. Heath, 1976.

C.K. Barrett, *The New Testament Background: Selected Documents*. San Francisco: Harper and Row, 1989.

Leon Bernard and Theodore B. Hodges, eds., *Readings in European History*. New York: Macmillan, 1958.

Henry Bettenson, ed., *Documents of the Christian Church*. London: Oxford University Press, 1967.

"Envoi: On Taking Leave of Antiquity," in John Boardman et al., eds., *The Oxford History of the Roman World*. New York: Oxford University Press, 1988.

Eusebius, *Ecclesiastical History*. 2 vols. Trans. Roy J. Deferrari. Washington, DC: Catholic University of America Press, 1955; also published as *The History of the Church*. Trans. G.A. Williamson, rev. Andrew Louth. New York: Penguin, 1989.

Holy Bible. Revised Standard Version. New York: Thomas Nelson and Sons, 1952.

Naphtali Lewis and Meyer Reinhold, eds., *Roman Civilization, Sourcebook 2: The Empire*. New York: Harper and Row, 1966.

Sister Mary Francis McDonald, trans., *Lactantius: Minor Works*. Washington, DC: Catholic University of America Press, 1965.

Alister E. McGrath, ed., *The Christian Theology Reader*. Oxford: Blackwell, 1995.

Wayne A. Meeks, ed., *The Writings of St. Paul*. New York: W.W. Norton, 1972.

Brian Tierney, ed., *The Middle Ages*. Vol. 1, *Sources of Medieval History*. New York: Knopf, 1973.

F.A. Wright, trans., *Select Letters of St. Jerome*. Cambridge, MA: Harvard University Press, 1963.

General Histories of Early Christianity

Henry Chadwick, *The Early Church*. Baltimore: Penguin Books, 1974.

Hans Conzelmann, *History of the Primitive Church*. Trans. John E. Steely. New York: Abingdon Press, 1973.

J.G. Davies, *The Early Christian Church*. Garden City, NY: Doubleday, 1967.

W.H.C. Frend, *The Early Church*. Philadelphia: Lippincott, 1966.

———, *The Rise of Christianity*. Philadelphia: Fortress Press, 1984.

Justo L. Gonzalez, *The Story of Christianity*. Vol. 1, *The Early Church to the Dawn of the Reformation*. San Francisco: Harper and Row, 1984.

Adolf Harnack, *The Mission and Expansion of Christianity in the First Three Centuries*. New York: Harper and Brothers, 1962.

Rodney Stark, *The Rise of Christianity: A Sociologist Reconsiders History*. Princeton, NJ: Princeton University Press, 1996.

J.W.C. Wand, *A History of the Early Church to A.D. 500*. London: Methuen, 1965.

Jewish Background of Christianity

Michael Baigent and Richard Leigh, *The Dead Sea Scrolls Deception*. New York: Summit Books, 1991.

James H. Charlesworth, ed., *Jesus and the Dead Sea Scrolls*. New York: Doubleday, 1992.

Max I. Dimont, *Jews, God and History*. New York: New American Library, 1962.

Robert Eisenman and Michael Wise, *The Dead Sea Scrolls Uncovered*. New York: Penguin Books, 1992.

Charles T. Fritsch, *The Qumran Community: Its History and Its Scrolls*. New York: Biblo and Tannen, 1972.

Michael Grant, *The Jews in the Roman World*. London: Weidenfeld and Nicolson, 1973.

Josephus, *The Jewish War*. Trans. G.A. Williamson. New York: Penguin Books, 1981.

Emil Schürer, *History of the Jewish People in the Age of Jesus*. Edinburgh: Clark, 1987.

Hershel Shanks, ed., *Understanding the Dead Sea Scrolls*. New York: Random House, 1992.

E.M. Smallwood, *The Jews Under Roman Rule*. Leiden: E.J. Brill, 1976.

James C. Vanderkam, *The Dead Sea Scrolls Today*. Grand Rapids: Willam B. Eerdmans, 1994.

Greco-Roman Setting of and Conflicts with Christianity

E.R. Dodds, *Pagan and Christian in an Age of Anxiety*. New York: Cambridge University Press, 1991.

Will Durant, *Caesar and Christ*. New York: Simon and Schuster, 1944.

Robin L. Fox, *Pagans and Christians*. San Francisco: HarperSanFrancisco, 1988.

Charles Freeman, *Egypt, Greece, and Rome*. New York: Oxford University Press, 1996.

W.H.C. Frend, *Martyrdom and Persecution in the Early Church*. Oxford: Blackwell, 1965.

Michael Grant, *History of Rome*. New York: Scribner's, 1978.

M.L.W. Laistner, *Christianity and Pagan Culture in the Later Roman Empire*. Ithaca, NY: Cornell University Press, 1951.

Ramsay MacMullen, *Christianizing the Roman Empire, A.D. 100–400*. New Haven, CT: Yale University Press, 1984.

Harold Mattingly, *Christianity in the Roman Empire*. New York: W.W. Norton, 1967.

Jaroslav Pelikan, *The Excellent Empire: The Fall of Rome and the Triumph of the Church*. San Francisco: Harper and Row, 1987.

Stewart Perowne, *Caesars and Saints: The Rise of the Christian State, A.D. 180–313*. New York: Barnes and Noble, 1992.

C. Thomas, *Christianity in Roman Britain to A.D. 500*. London: Batsford, 1981.

Paul Veyne, ed., *From Pagan Rome to Byzantium*. Vol. 1 of Philippe Ariès and Georges Duby, eds., *A History of Private Life*. Cambridge, MA: Harvard University Press, 1987.

Robert L. Wilken, *The Christians as the Romans Saw Them*. New Haven, CT: Yale University Press, 1984.

Christ, the Apostles, and Paul

James H. Charlesworth, ed., *Jesus Within Judaism: New Light from Exciting Archaeological Discoveries*. New York: Doubleday, 1988.

John D. Crossan, *The Historical Jesus: The Life of a Mediterranean Jewish Peasant*. San Francisco: HarperCollins, 1992.

Leonhard Goppelt, *Jesus, Paul, and Judaism*. New York: Thomas Nelson and Sons, 1964.

Michael Grant, *Jesus: An Historian's View of the Gospels*. New York: Scribner's, 1977.

Roberta L. Harris, *The World of the Bible*. New York: Thames and Hudson, 1995.

Joseph Klausner, *Jesus of Nazareth*. New York: Menorah Press, 1978.

Jacques Maritain, *Living Thoughts of St. Paul*. New York: Longmans, 1941.

Paul W. Roberts, *In Search of the Birth of Jesus*. New York: Riverhead Books, 1995.

John Romer, *Testament: The Bible and History*. New York: Henry Holt, 1988.

E.P. Sanders, *The Historical Figure of Jesus*. New York: Penguin Books, 1993.

A.N. Wilson, *Jesus*. London: Sinclair-Stevenson, 1992.

———, *Paul: The Mind of the Apostle*. New York: W.W. Norton, 1997.

Constantine and the Christians

Timothy D. Barnes, *Constantine and Eusebius*. Cambridge, MA: Harvard University Press, 1981.

Norman H. Baynes, *Constantine the Great and the Christian Church*. London: Oxford University Press, 1972.

Michael Grant, *Constantine the Great: The Man and His Times*. New York: Scribner's, 1994.

A.H.M. Jones, *Constantine and the Conversion of Europe*. Toronto: University of Toronto Press, 1978.

Ramsay MacMullen, *Constantine*. New York: Dial Press, 1969.

Social, Cultural, and Literary Aspects of Early Christianity

P. Brown, *Religion and Society in the Age of Saint Augustine*. London: Faber and Faber, 1972.

Peter R. Brown, *Augustine of Hippo: A Biography*. Berkeley and Los Angeles: University of California Press, 1967.

Charles Freeman, *The World of the Romans*. New York: Oxford University Press, 1993.

Michael Gough, *The Origins of Christian Art*. London: Thames and Hudson, 1973.

Tony Lane, *Exploring Christian Thought*. Nashville: Thomas Nelson and Sons, 1984.

W.A. Meeks, *The First Urban Christians: The Social World of the Apostle Paul*. New Haven, CT: Yale University Press, 1983.

Jaroslav Pelikan, *Christianity and Classical Culture*. New Haven, CT: Yale University Press, 1993.

J. Stevenson, *The Catacombs: Rediscovered Monuments of Early Christianity*. London: Thames and Hudson, 1978.

Marina Warner, *Alone of Her Sex: The Myth and the Cult of the Virgin Mary*. New York: Random House, 1976.

Later Development and Overall Impact of Christianity

Owen Chadwick, *A History of Christianity*. New York: St. Martin's Press, 1995.

Stewart C. Easton, *The Western Heritage*. New York: Holt, Rinehart, and Winston, 1970.

Paul Johnson, *A History of Christianity*. New York: Atheneum, 1980.

C. Harold King, *A History of Civilization: Earliest Times to the Mid–Seventeenth Century*. New York: Scribner's, 1964.

Kenneth S. Latourette, *A History of Christianity*. New York: Harper and Brothers, 1953.

David Nicholas, *The Medieval West, 400–1450: A Preindustrial Civilization*. Homewood, IL: Dorsey Press, 1973.

Robert Payne, *The Christian Centuries: From Christ to Dante*. New York: W.W. Norton, 1966.

Bruce L. Shelley, *Church History in Plain Language*. Dallas: Word Publishing, 1995.

Howard F. Vos, *Introduction to Church History*. Nashville: Thomas Nelson and Sons, 1994.

Index

02

H Williams	
10/19/09	

DATE DUE